WALES AND THE AIR WAR 1914–1918

ALAN PHILLIPS

AMBERLEY

First published 2015

Amberley Publishing
The Hill, Stroud
Gloucestershire, GL5 4EP

www.amberley-books.com

Copyright © Alan Phillips, 2015

The right of Alan Phillips to be identified as the Author
of this work has been asserted in accordance with the
Copyrights, Designs and Patents Act 1988.

All rights reserved. No part of this book may be reprinted
or reproduced or utilised in any form or by any electronic,
mechanical or other means, now known or hereafter invented,
including photocopying and recording, or in any information
storage or retrieval system, without the permission in writing
from the Publishers.

British Library Cataloguing in Publication Data.
A catalogue record for this book is available from the British Library.

ISBN 978 1 4456 5219 1 (print)
ISBN 978 1 4456 5220 7 (ebook)

Typeset in 10pt on 13pt Sabon.
Typesetting and Origination by Amberley Publishing.
Printed in the UK.

Contents

Chapter 1	An Introduction to the First World War	5
Chapter 2	Formation of the Air Wings	13
Chapter 3	Airships Campaign Against the U-boat	17
Chapter 4	Land-Based Aircraft Contribution	41
Chapter 5	The Seaplane Offensive	51
Chapter 6	Flying Training in Wales During the First World War	65
Chapter 7	Welsh Air Bases During the First World War	69
Appendix I	Aircraft Used During the First World War	79
Appendix II	List of Personnel Based in Wales	91
	Acknowledgements	93
	Bibliography	95

Chapter 1

An Introduction to the First World War

When the First World War broke out in August 1914, emphasis was put on recruiting able-bodied men to join the army. The established military training camps became overwhelmed with eager young men wanting to join up. New camps had to be built and it was inevitable that areas in Wales were chosen as locations for military bases.

Europe had erupted into a world war the likes of which no one had ever seen before, initially involving several countries and eventually embroiling every family, every hamlet, every village and town in the land one way or the other. Thousands upon thousands of young men eagerly joined up answering Kitchener's call: 'Your Country Needs You', many of whom would never see their home or country again. Groups of lads from a particular village joined up together and sadly died together. With the young able-bodied men away at war, the women became the workers of Britain in all sorts of factories, and especially dealing with munitions.

A Willows Balloon in 1910. E. T. Willows' design influenced airships used during the war.

Throughout August and September 1914 there was an unprecedented level of activity throughout Wales as the country prepared for war. Local Yeomanry were mustered almost immediately and put on standby.

In 1914, Wales was not regarded as an ideal part of the country for establishing any type of airfield because of its rugged terrain and its distance from where the action was. The authorities' first priority was building up the army to a reasonable strength to face the German onslaught.

It was inevitable that certain parts of Wales would eventually be chosen as locations for airfields and military bases in time of emergency. Several ports and harbours had already become important bases for warships.

Official records of the air war in Wales are often sketchy and, as aerial activity over the country was minimal, very little was reported in local newspapers. However, when an aircraft or an airship appeared over an area or a town it was worthy of a mention, provided it was not censored.

Being an island nation, the United Kingdom has always had the advantage of being surrounded by the sea, which has been a natural defence against any invader. However, in the twentieth century there was a different sort of threat, although the threat of sea invasion still remained to a certain degree.

From the early twentieth century, the United Kingdom had depended on commerce; the whole wealth of the nation relied on its imports and exports. The interception of commercial shipping was regarded as fair game in a time of conflict for any nation possessing ships. This was incredibly clear during conflicts in previous centuries.

Before the war, several early aviators flew demonstration flights throughout Wales. Crowds have gathered around Robert Loraine's biplane at Rhos-on-Sea in 1910.

Another demonstration flight that drew great interest was the Avro Waterplane at Llandudno in 1914.

The Royal Navy possessed the largest and most modern fleet in the world and was considered capable of protecting all the vital sea routes for commercial shipping. Coastal defences from the Gower Peninsula to Pembrokeshire, and from Gwynedd to Flint, were beefed up and manned. Old forts dating back to the Napoleonic wars were reactivated and manned. Before the end of the year, tented army camps emerged in almost every county.

In the early part of the war the greatest threat to the British coast and shipping was warships of the German Hochseeflotte (High Seas Fleet). It began its shipping attacks in the traditional way, by using its surface raiders, mostly cruisers, where the Allied naval forces were at their weakest. Within months, the German cruisers and raiders were hunted down by the Royal Navy and sunk. Others were blockaded in their home ports with the rest of the German High Seas Fleet.

The German U-boat was the biggest threat to shipping throughout the First World War.

A new threat emerged to shipping and that was the German U-boat, which was capable of slipping out of the German bases undetected and harassing British shipping around the coast and beyond.

The First World War U-boat campaign began on 4 February 1915, when the German High Command announced that shipping in the vicinity of Britain and Ireland was a legitimate target. Up to then only warships of Britain and France had been targeted by enemy submarines and surface ships. However, concessions were made due to American (who were then neutral) pressure that all ships flying flags of a neutral country and hospital ships were exempted.

During the war, enemy submarines took a heavy toll on Allied shipping in every theatre of the war. It began with the gentlemanlike principle of evacuating civilians before sinking the ship, but it soon developed into torpedoing the cargo ship without warning.

The shipping lanes around the Welsh coast were of the utmost importance to the war effort of the British Isles in the imports of essential food and raw material for industry. Various areas of the country relied on coastal shipping as most of the coal from south and north coal fields were shipped by coastal freighters. Welsh coal was the main power source for the Royal Navy ships based around the UK before conversion to oil.

Just as the Irish Sea, St George's Channel and Liverpool Bay were to the north, with its ports of Belfast, Holyhead, Liverpool and the industrial areas of Merseyside, the Bristol Channel and the South Western approaches were high risk areas as they were on the sea routes to the important south Wales and the West Country ports. Later, these same ports and areas would be subjected to the highest protection during the Second World War.

The war began badly on number of fronts and especially with mounting shipping losses. The coast and shipping lanes around Wales were classed as a war zone and became the graveyard of many ships. It was on 4 February 1915 that the full U-boat attacks became obvious around the coast of Wales.

A copy of Willy Stower's painting of *U-21* capturing the SS *Linda Blanche* on 30 January 1915.

SS *Bengrove*, which was torpedoed off Ilfracombe on 7 March 1915. (Courtesy of Wrecksite)

Airship patrols were urgently required in the area when, in 1915, six merchant ships were sunk off the northern coast of Wales. The largest sunk was SS *Hartdale*, a 3,839-ton cargo ship bound for Alexandria in Egypt, by *U-27* 7 miles south-east of South Rock. The SS *Linda Blanche*, belonging to the Anglesey Shipping Company, was captured and scuttled by *U-21* north-west by north of the Liverpool Bar light ship on its passage between Manchester and Belfast on 30 January 1915. Shipping losses in the south Wales area were very high. The SS *Mikasa* was sunk on 13 January at Woody Bay in the Bristol Channel. The 2,398-ton collier SS *Bengrove*, sailing out of Barry with 5,000 tons of coal, was torpedoed some 5 miles NNE of Ilfracombe on Sunday 7 March 1915. The ship's explosion was witnessed from the shore by several people; initially it was thought it had hit a mine but it later was claimed by *U-20*. Over the next few months, the tally of ships sunk in the Bristol Channel continued to grow. The SS *Morwenna*, sailing from Cardiff to Sydney, was captured and sunk by *U-41* off St Anne's Head off the coast of Pembrokeshire on 26 May 1915. A day before, the *Victoria* out of Milford was also attacked and sunk off St Anne's Head. On 15 June, en route from Penarth to Archangel, SS *Strathnairn* was sunk by *U-22* some 25 miles north-east of Bishop and Clerks rocks off Ramsey Island. SS *Dumfrieshire* was torpedoed and sank off the Smalls (off the coast of Pembrokeshire) on 28 June. Another was SS *Rosalie*, a 4,242-ton cargo ship, which was sunk on 22 August.

These are only a small example of ships lost during the period. The greatest loss of life to occur in Welsh waters was on 10 October 1918 with the sinking in the Irish Sea of the morning mail boat RMS *Leinster City*, which belonged to the Dublin Steam Packet Company. The Kingstown (Dun Laoghaire) to Holyhead ferry was struck by two torpedoes fired by *U-123* off the Kish Bank. The ship sank in 20 minutes, with the loss of 501 passengers and crew out of a complement of 771. Most of the passengers were military personnel returning to duty from leave.

The German U-boat was not truly defeated, but the Allies were able to keep the menace under control and provide protection for the ships. However, even after the convoy system was introduced with naval escorts and air patrols, in eighteen months 1,300 merchant ships were sunk in the Atlantic and in home waters. Three quarters of the merchant ships lost in 1917–18 were sunk 50 miles off the coast of Britain and France. Four out of every ten were even only 10 miles off the coast, usually in sight of land.

In the early years of the war, the Admiralty believed that only warships were capable of protecting the sea lanes from German surface raiders and U-boats. Admittedly, at the time the aeroplane was in its infancy and was not regarded as a potential contender in fighting U-boats, but in a short amount of time there were massive improvements and increased reliability in aircraft design. As was so often the case, a warship took a considerable amount of time to reach a stricken ship or a periscope sighting, whereas an aircraft could be on site a lot sooner.

This was the logical thinking that changed the Admiralty view of the aeroplane, which consequently brought the development of airships and aircraft to the forefront, especially for maritime use.

Although the air war had raged in the skies over the Western Front since 1914, it wasn't until 1915 that it came to Wales when the Admiralty approved the building of two air stations in the country, one on Anglesey and the other in Pembrokeshire.

SS *Leinster* was torpedoed with heavy loss of life on 10 October 1918. (Courtesy of the Holyhead Museum)

The country had witnessed the establishment of army recruitment camps throughout the country since the outbreak of war, which was soon followed by the stationing of Royal Navy warships at Welsh ports. However, the air war was something new. Previously, few people had had the privilege of encountering an aeroplane, usually during the flying demonstrations held prior to the outbreak of war. People living in the vicinity of Milton and Llangefni soon witnessed a war that had up to then seemed so far away, and was now in their backyards with the airships and aircraft taking off on patrols.

Some Welsh firms became heavily involved in war work. On the aviation side the Willows Aircraft Company of Cardiff built barrage balloons, while the Cambrian Aircraft Corporation of East Moors, Cardiff, built components for aircraft such as the DH.10.

Wales never experienced the Zeppelin raids that certain parts of southern and eastern England had to endure; although some towns in south Wales were put on blackout notifications, these were not implemented.

From the very beginning, total war took a firm grip on Wales just as it did throughout the rest of the United Kingdom. Surprisingly, support for the conflict was massive right up to the end, even when the young men who left their homes and villages never returned. A generation had been decimated, but the nation survived and was determined to make better future. They really believed that this was a war to end all wars.

A Sea Scout Zero Class airship overflying a convoy.

Chapter 2

Formation of the Air Wings

It was not long before it became evident that aircraft would play an important part in the forthcoming conflict. At first these flimsy flying machines were only used for observation and reconnaissance, working in co-operation with observation balloons. Initially, both sides fired their pistols and rifles at each other but later machine guns were fitted. As more sophisticated designs became available, the flying machine was found to be a very formidable weapon of war.

At the outbreak of the First World War, the main contenders' air strength was similar in many respects; France only had 140 flying machines and a number of observation balloons. Germany had a similar number of aircraft, most of which were inferior to the French. Britain's total air strength in August 1914 was a pitiful sight of only 113 aircraft, most of which were civilian and taken over by the military, none of which were built for any sort of combat and which became easy prey to enemy aircraft. The core of the country's military flying element was the early pioneer aviators who eventually trained pilots for the services.

As the conflict progressed the government concluded that to dominate the air over the battle area, new aircraft was required. As a matter of urgency, initially only the proven pre-war designs were built, therefore contracts were awarded to various companies throughout the United Kingdom, not necessarily firms with flying know-how but companies with ample floor space for manufacturing. This gave an opportunity for the aircraft companies to concentrate on developing new designs for the services.

As the war progressed, new improved designs appeared and were rushed into service. Flimsy biplanes with top speeds of 30–50 mph gave way to fighters capable of 130 mph. Engine power increased threefold, which also increased the aircraft's fire power and bomb load. By the end of the war, twin-engine bombers could fly great distances to drop bombs on their enemy.

In Britain, the Army first got involved with manufacturing lighter-than-air flying machines when the Army Balloon Equipment Store of the Royal Engineers was formed at Woolwich in 1878. A balloon section, with its own factory and training school, was formed at Chatham and later moved to Aldershot in 1902. In 1911, the balloon section became the Air Battalion, based at Farnborough.

Up until the formation of the RFC on 13 March 1912, Britain's air element consisted of an Air Battalion comprised of two companies – No. 1 Company with airships and balloons, and No. 2 with aircraft.

Wales and the Air War 1914–1918

Drawings of badges and cap badges of the different services.

In 1908, the British government became concerned about the development of airships on the Continent and their potential threat to the country. To analyse the threat closely, the Admiralty decided that Vickers, Sons & Maxim Ltd at Barrow-in-Furness should design and build a rigid airship. The airship, known as Rigid Naval Airship No. 1 and named *Mayfly*, emerged from the shed on 22 May 1911.

The Royal Navy had been conducting numerous trials with rigid airships since 1911, but these were used mostly for fleet observation from naval warships. In September 1911, the navy also conducted several trials with aircraft fitted with floats. These trials continued on and off until the outbreak of the war in 1914.

One such trial was conducted at Dale in Pembrokeshire in 1912 with what was referred to as a hydroplane. Initial testing proved disappointing but was resumed again with the approval of the Admiralty in August 1913. The aircraft were a Burney X2 and X3, designed and built by the Bristol & Colonial Aeroplane Company of Bristol. Once again early tests were disappointing, but the first flight took place in October.

On 13 May 1912, two separate air wings were formed within the RFC: a naval and military wing.

With the backing of Winston Churchill as the First Lord of the Admiralty, the naval wing became the Royal Naval Air Service in July 1914 with ninety-three aircraft of various type, six airships, two balloons and 727 personnel.

At the outbreak of the First World War, the military wing of the RFC went to France to support the British expeditionary force with just sixty-three various aircraft, 105 officers and ninety-five motor transport.

The RNAS were given the task of defending the homeland against any hostile attacks, from the air or the sea. Although as the war progressed the RNAS took some offensive action in Germany against the Zeppelin sheds, their main responsibility was home defence, which included defending British cities from Zeppelin attacks. These attacks were concentrated on the south-east coast and the eastern side of the country – even parts of Scotland were attacked. As the air raids on towns involved in the war effort continued and casualties grew, special emphasis was put on the RFC and RNAS to provide home defence flights for the targeted areas. Wales was fortunate that no Zeppelin raids occurred; this was mostly because any flight over mainland Britain would be too risky, although the airship had the range to do so. Therefore, there was no need for home defence airstrips to be constructed. The RNAS bases in Wales concentrated on coastal defence against the U-boats, which were causing havoc on coastal shipping.

Throughout the war both services' equipment improved and increased, and as new aircraft reached the front line, the older and obsolescent equipment was withdrawn and used for training and secondary duties. Coastal patrol duties, or maritime reconnaissance as it became known, was considered the Cinderella of the air campaign during both world wars due to making do with outdated equipment. But, due to their bravery and determination, personnel from the various squadrons did sterling work in both wars.

The Royal Air Force was formed on 1 April 1918 by amalgamating the Royal Flying Corps and the Royal Naval Air Service to become what is now the oldest independent air force in the world.

At the time of the amalgamation of the two air wings, it was only seen as a temporary arrangement for the duration of the war. Lord Trenchard, Chief of the Air Staff, wrote in 1919, 'The whole service was practically a war creation on a temporary basis.' As time went on he realised it was going to be a permanent solution and the Royal Air Force was there to stay.

Day to day operations at the bases remained the same although the RNAS was abolished on 1 April. All personnel kept their Royal Navy rank and naval traditions. The airships remained the property of the Admiralty well after April 1918 and were not transferred to Air Ministry control until the cessation of hostilities.

Due to a shortage of manpower, the services relied on women to fill important roles in all three services. In December 1917, the Royal Flying Corp began recruiting women directly rather than as a secondment from the WAAC and in February 1918, the Women's Royal Naval Air Service was formed. The women were able to fill most jobs done by the men; they were drivers, workshop mechanics, w/t operators etc.

In Wales, women of the naval air service were stationed at Bangor, Llangefni, Milton and Fishguard, and were usually supplemented by civilian household staff.

At the end of the First World War, the Royal Air Force was the largest such force in the world with 291,000 officers and other ranks, possessing over 200 squadrons and 22,647 aircraft.

Demobilisation brought a drastic reduction in the RAF's strength; within eighteen months, personnel had been reduced to 27,000. The service lost the majority of its air crew and experienced and skilled mechanics, some of whom joined the numerous air charter companies and the small airlines that started with the availability of surplus military aircraft. Even then, after the drastic cuts the RAF was still the largest independent air force in the world.

Chapter 3

Airships Campaign Against the U-boat

As an island nation, Britain has always been dependent on its sea lanes for trade and the import of valuable commodities, especially during times of war and conflict.

This became incredibly apparent during the First World War when enemy ships, especially submarines, attacked and sank ships supplying the United Kingdom's needs.

Initially only warships had been targeted by enemy submarines and surface warships. However, on 4 February 1915 the rules changed when the German High Command announced that any vessels in the vicinity of Britain and Ireland were legitimate targets for its submarines. All the shipping lanes around the coast of the British Isles became prime targets for the U-boats and surface vessels, and as several sea lanes were in the vicinity of the Welsh coastline, the country was soon to play an important part in protecting the convoys.

Pembrokeshire, a county not facing the Continent, nevertheless commanded the south-western approaches to Britain and to south Wales' ports of Barry, Cardiff, Llanelli and Swansea, which were key locations for conveying coal to other parts of the country. Several coastal ships (colliers) were sunk either by direct encounters with U-boats or by mines laid by submarines. In the north-west, Liverpool was one of the main ports in the British Isles and drew a considerable interest from the enemy; within weeks of the announcement, three ships were sunk off Liverpool and a further two more were sunk off the north Welsh coast.

During this period, several ships sailing in the Irish Sea reported sighting submarine periscopes; even a German surface vessel was reported.

The most formidable deterrent against submarines was warships armed with depth charges, but the response time was not ideal. The time from when a submarine was sighted to the time that a warship would reach the scene could be several hours at best, and by then the ship had been sunk and the submarine was on its way home.

The only solution to the menace was an aircraft, something the Admiralty had been aware of since a conference held on 24 February, when the danger of attack by submarines on shipping and ways of meeting such attacks were discussed. In 1915 there were no suitable aircraft available for the task with sufficient endurance for sea patrols, nor any that had the capability or reliability, so the airship filled the gap.

For some years the Admiralty had been using various dirigibles for fleet patrols that operated from ships and shore bases, and found they had remarkable endurance providing

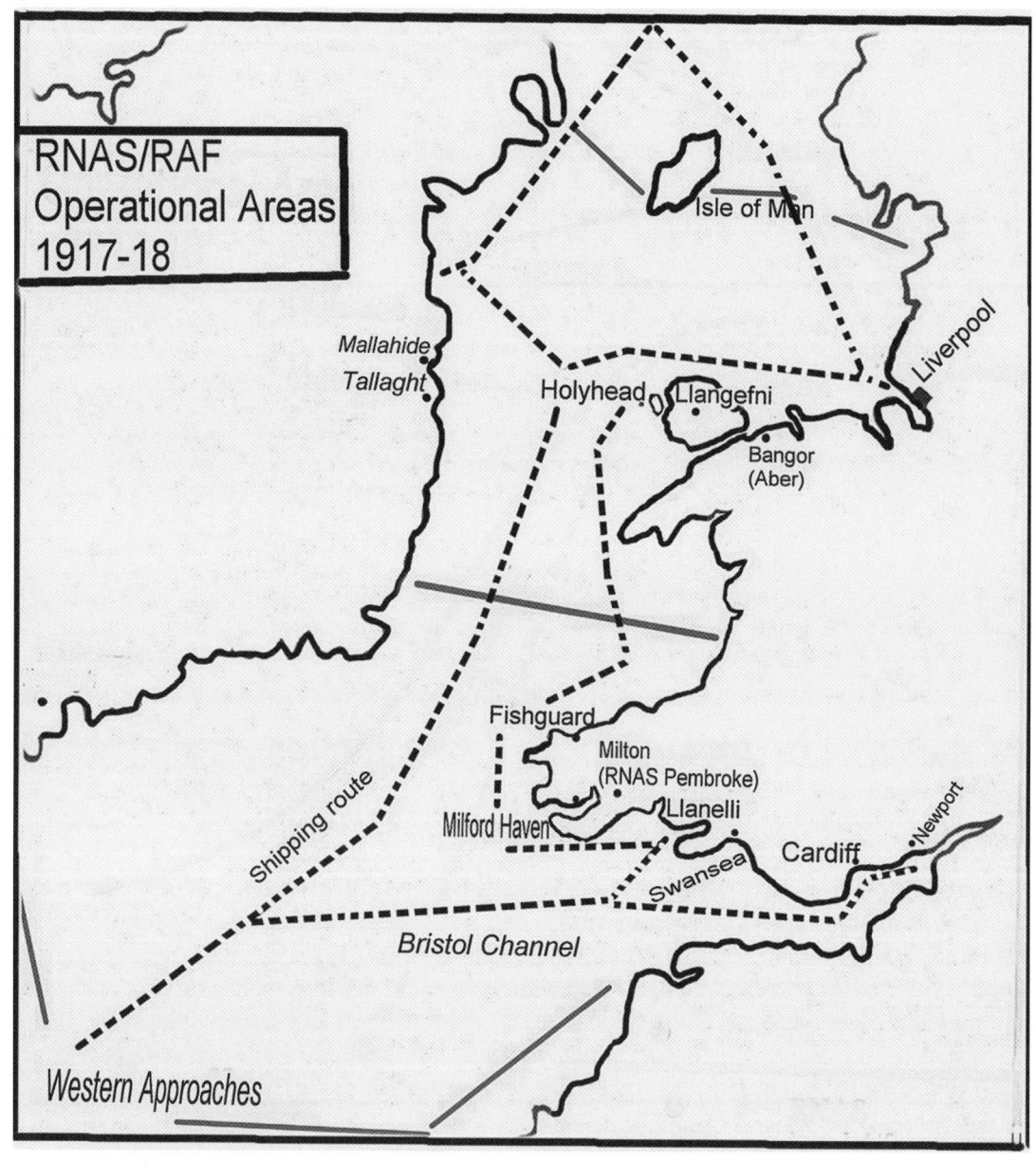

Map showing RNAS Anglesey and Pembroke patrol areas. (Alan Phillips Collection)

the weather was fine. After numerous experiments and modification at Farnborough, several airships were armed and adapted for sea patrols. Eventually the Sea Scout type went into limited production.

To accommodate the airships, the Admiralty built a number of air stations throughout the British Isles. Two of these were built: one in north Wales at Anglesey, with a subsidiary station at Malahide outside Dublin, and one at Milton in the south of Pembrokeshire, with a subsidiary at Killeugh, Cork, in Ireland.

Aerial view of RNAS Anglesey airship station. (Courtesy of the Royal Air Force Museum)

Some of RNAS Anglesey's personnel posing outside the officers' mess. (Anglesey Archives)

In Pembrokeshire the Admiralty acquired 228 acres of land near the villages of Milton and Sageston, just off the main road between Pembroke and Carmarthen, with the intention of building an airship base, which became RNAS Pembroke.

The island of Anglesey was first suggested as a site for an airship station. Several sites on the island were considered but eventually 200-plus acres of farmland on high ground some 3 miles from the town of Llangefni were acquired.

The Llangefni patrol sector covered an area from Bardsey Island to Dublin and up as far as the Isle of Man and Morecambe Bay, which included the entrance to Liverpool docks.

Llangefni airship station (RNAS Anglesey) was commissioned on 26 September 1915 as part of No. 14 Group, which was responsible for the protection of the British coastline. The station's first commanding officer was Major George Scott, who eventually became Deputy Director of Airship Development, but tragically lost his life in the R101 crash in France in 1930.

Major Scott billeted at the Bull Hotel, Llangefni, and he and his men became well known in the town, some more often for their drunkenness and boisterous behavior.

Airship patrols were urgently required in an attempt to reduce the high shipping losses. The first airship to be based at Llangefni was Sea Scout No. 18, crewed by Flight Sub-Lieutenants W. Urquart and Kilburn, which was flown in from Kingsnorth on 26 September. However, SS-18 was seriously damaged on 9 October 1916 during an attempted landing: it struck a cow in an adjoining field, damaging the control car and rendering the airship uncontrollable. The observer was thrown out of the forward

Sea Scout Class airships were first based at Anglesey. Photo of a Llangefni-based SS-24 landing.

cockpit but only suffered minor injuries. The lightened airship flew upwards and drifted out to sea with the Captain, Flight Sub-Lieutenant Arthur Donald Thompson, and the flight engineer just helpless passengers. The pilot eventually managed to open the gas valve, releasing the hydrogen from the balloon. The airship came down heavy off the coast of Ireland on 22 October, causing the fuselage to split in half and throw the flight engineer into the sea where he unfortunately drowned. Luckily, Arthur Thompson clung to the wrecked car and was rescued by a passing steamer.

The next airship to arrive at Llangefni was SS-22 with a BE2c car on 5 November 1915, captained by F/Sub-Lieutenant E. F. Turner. SS-22's claim to fame was that it achieved the diving record for descending from 1,100 feet to 100 feet in 56 seconds, which was an exceptional performance for an airship of the day. SS-22 left Llangefni for Wormwood Scrubs in April 1917 and was eventually handed over to the Italian navy on 2 June 1917.

Also in 1915, SS-24 (with a BE2c car) arrived at RNAS Anglesey, captained by Sub Lieutenant Scroggs. The airship remained at Llangefni; it flew patrols and convoy protection until 11 July 1917 when it departed for Luce Bay for patrol work in the North Channel. It was eventually decommissioned in July 1918.

The Anglesey-based Sea Scouts had a reasonable safety record, but mishaps did occasionally happen, such as with SS-25.

SS-25 was another airship to land at Llangefni in 1915, captained by Sub-Lieutenant T. B. Williams. Returning from a long patrol on 23 November 1917, it made a forced landing and was badly damaged. The crew followed landing procedure by dropping grapnels and trailing ropes but still landed very heavily, crashing through some trees and

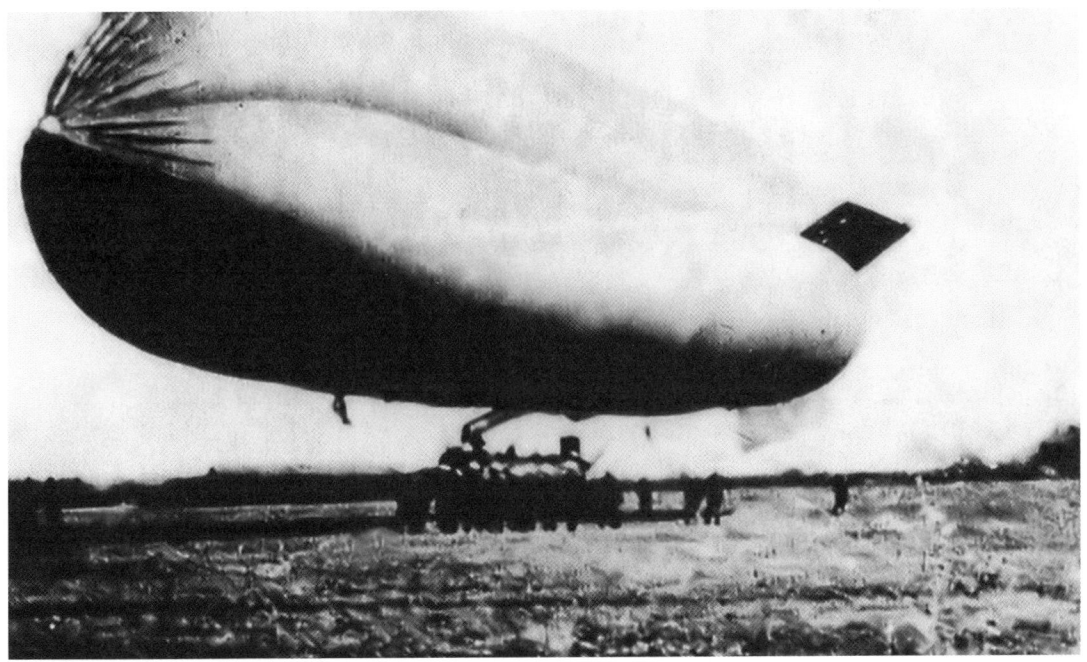

A rare visitor to RNAS Anglesey was the large Coastal Class.

A Sea Scout Zero Class taking off from Anglesey.

damaging the car and controls. One consolation was that airships were easily repaired and usually returned to action quickly. SS-25 flew a total of 149 hours between August and December 1917 and seventy-seven hours in 1918 before the Armistice.

Sub-Lieutenant T. B. Williams was involved in experiments to improve the performance of the SS-Class airships during July and November in 1916 Kingsnorth prior to his posting to RNAS Anglesey.

Within weeks, a full complement of four Sea Scout airships had arrived at the station, completing the initial establishment, and began escorting the Liverpool-bound convoys and the Dublin–Holyhead ferry.

RNAS Anglesey received its last Sea Scout on 4 November 1916 – SS-33 with a Maurice Farman car was built at Vickers Ltd in Barrow in January 1916. The airship came from Luce Bay to relieve the over-worked Llangefni crews. However, during a convoy patrol in April 1917 it was forced to land at Cemlyn Bay due to engine failure, but only sustained slight damage.

The Admiralty continually experimented with ways of combating the U-boats and tracing their whereabouts. The most interesting were experiments with hydrophones, basically an underwater microphone that was lowered from an airship into the sea to detect sounds from a submarine electric engine. During a lull in patrols and escort duties, both RNAS Anglesey and Pembroke were involved with the experiment. Although it was never used during the First World War, it has proved invaluable for underwater detection since.

After a mishap on patrol, SS-25 is being towed back to Holyhead by the ship *Amethyst*.

A Sea Scout Zero airship being manhandled by ground staff prior to take off. (F. Thomas)

A close-up of SS Zero's fuselage.

In Pembrokeshire, the base at Milton did not take shape until early January/February 1916; it was very similar in construction to Llangefni but with two 120 foot × 318 foot corrugated iron hangars, together with large windshields. Two lots of hydrogen storage tanks were constructed adjacent to the hangars. Wooden huts and canvas workshops were constructed, as well as a number of tented accommodations for the personnel. In April 1916, RNAS Pembroke was classed as fully operational.

During the early months of 1916, the base became mostly a stopping point for airships attached to various warships patrolling the Irish Sea. This arrangement was quite useful to Milton personnel as it gave them considerable training in handling the crafts.

The first airship to arrive at Pembroke was SS-15 with a BE2c car (cupola) on 25 April 1916. The airship was built at Wormwood Scrubs in August 1915. SS-15 operated out of Pembroke on shipping patrols and U-boat searches in the Bristol Channel and south-western approaches. On one such patrol on 18 January 1917 it ran into bad weather and was wrecked off Lundy island.

Another SS to arrive at Pembroke for trials was SS-42 on 28 August 1916. While landing after a routine patrol, on 15 September 1916 the airship broke away from its moorings in a strong gust with the pilot, Flight Lieutenant Errol F. Monk, aboard. The airship lifted some 30 feet in the air, crashing to the ground on its port side and damaging and breaking most of the suspension cables and damaging the car. The wireless operator fell 20 feet to the ground, leaving Monk hanging on to the airship as it climbed

Right: Llangefni-based airship flying over Caernarfon Castle.

Below: The crew of a Llangefni-based Zero airship making final checks. (Courtesy of R. Sloan)

An aerial view of RNAS Pembroke, taken from an airship in 1918. (Courtesy FAAM)

uncontrollably. SS-42 flew for 100 miles towards Lundy island and rose at one point to the height of 8,400 feet, with the pilot hanging on for dear life on the undercarriage. It eventually crashed at Ivybridge, Devon.

Flight Lieutenant Monk was badly injured with a fractured spine, but made a speedy recovery and returned to duty ten months later.

The Sea Scout airships had been hurriedly developed by the Admiralty to counter the U-boat threat to shipping. It was realised that the SSs were just a stopgap with limited capabilities. A larger airship was required with greater range and endurance, twin engines for reliability and capable of carrying more armament. The Coastal Class was developed by using two Avro 510 seaplane fuselages joined together. The four-cockpit car was powered by two 150 hp Sunbeam engines on either end, one a tractor, the other a pusher. The first trial flight took place on 26 May 1915 from Kingsnorth. Over the preceding months several modifications were made, including upgrading the Sunbeam engines. Fully loaded, the Coastals could carry half a ton of bombs or depth charges for twelve hours. Maximum speed was 46 mph and they had an endurance of nearly twenty hours. The airship was armed with two .303 Lewis machine guns.

It was soon realised that the Coastal types would be more beneficial based at Pembroke as its patrol area extended into the western approaches.

The first Coastal to be based at Pembroke was C-6, which arrived by rail from Kingsnorth on 29 May 1916. The airship arrived in crates at Haverforwest rail station and was transported by road to RNAS Pembroke. Within a week the airship was operational and began convoy patrols and anti-submarine sweeps in the Irish Sea and

Coastal Class C-3 at Pembroke, being prepared for take-off. (Courtesy of C. Mowthorpe)

Coastal C-6 at RNAS Pembroke. (Via FFA)

the western approaches. The sight of the Coastal airships to the weary convoys turning the southern coast of Ireland was very reassuring as no ship was ever attacked or sunk when airships were present. The second Coastal Class (C-3) arrived at RNAS Pembroke on 9 June. One of the first actions involving a C-type was in November 1916 when C-6 dropped two small bombs on a possible periscope sighting east of Cork. During another long patrol in poor weather, C-6 had to make a forced landing at Germag, near Mullion, on 2 December 1916, but returned to Pembroke after slight repairs. C-6's last patrol was on 23 March 1917; at the end of a long eleven-hour patrol it developed engine trouble and crashed into the sea with no survivors.

The last of the Coastal type (C-5A) arrived at RNAS Pembroke for trials on 27 August 1917 after being reassembled following an incident at Longside in January, when the carriage was totally destroyed. It remained at Pembroke until 24 March 1918, where it had accumulated over 605 hours on patrols and convoy duties.

During 1917, enemy submarine activity around Wales had increased considerably. In February alone six coastal vessels were sunk near Bardsey Island, which caused some concern in the Admiralty and put extra pressure on RNAS Anglesey to combat the threat.

Two Coastal Class airships at RNAS Pembroke in 1917.

Another Coastal based at Pembroke was C-4.

In June 1917, most of the SS series were replaced by the Mark 2, which was known as a Sea Scout Pusher airship. These types had an increased gas volume, over 70,000 cubic feet, and a crew of three. Only six of the type were built, three of which replaced the older type at Llangefni.

The first to be based at Anglesey was SSP-5 on 18 January 1917 from Wormwood Scrubs. Previously, the airship, together with SSP-2, was modified to take a black envelope (85,000 cubic feet) and fitted with a silenced engine for secret night flights in France. SSP-6 arrived at RNAS Anglesey on 16 June 1917, also from Wormwood Scrubs; the charismatic T. B. Williams piloted it. During its stay at Llangefni it logged 320 hours. While on patrol on 16 March 1918, the airship crash-landed in the Irish Sea with engine trouble. Fortunately for the crew they were picked up by a passing ship, and the airship was taken in tow. Being lighter and in tow, the airship took to the air, just like when running with a kite, consequently cutting the towrope and floating south-eastwards. It flew over mid-Wales and eventually landed in a wood in Chichester, Sussex. The envelope was deflated and returned to Llangefni. On 12 April 1918, SSP-6 was to partake in training at the airship training centre at RNAS Cranwell, but another engine failure meant that it was forced to land near Blackburn and was badly damaged. The last SSP to arrive at Llangefni was SSP-1 on 5 July 1917 from Kingsnorth; this airship's claim to fame was it could attain 52 mph in flight.

As a refueling point during the long airship patrols, a mooring station was built at Malahide near Dublin and at Killeaugh, County Cork, which allowed the airship not

Close-up of Coastal Class fuselage, fully armed. (Via C. Mowthorpe)

only an opportunity to refuel and rearm, but also gave a short respite for the crew during their long patrols.

In 1917, twenty-seven ships were sunk by German U-boats in the patrol area of RNAS Anglesey and Pembroke. Mines laid by U-boats claimed several ships along the Welsh coast right up until the end of the war, some even after the Armistice, such as SS *Lucia*, which struck a mine laid by *UC-65* off St David's Head on 11 February 1917.

The Admiralty was constantly searching for the ultimate patrolling airship and, after various classes, developed and built the Submarine Scout Zero type. This was the reason for the limited production of the successful SSP Class.

The SS Zero was a non-rigid airship with a total volume of 70,000 cubic feet. The beam was 30 feet and overall height 44 feet 6 inches. Length of carriage was over 18 feet. Total fuel capacity was 102 gallons, which gave it an endurance of sixteen hours at 50 mph, or forty hours at 20 mph. It had a crew of three in a modified B.E.20 fuselage.

Although the SS Zero Class was issued to most air stations, SS-42 was rebuilt at Wormwood Scrubs and returned to Pembroke as SS-42A in August 1917 to supplement the other airship based at the station. Unfortunately, the airship was involved yet again in an incident on 12 September when it crashed into some farmyard buildings during a night landing. The crew, F/Sub Lieutenant Cripps and his wireless operator, were unable to abandon the craft; it drifted out to sea in the direction of Carmarthen Bay and was wrecked near Bull Point. Both crewmembers lost their lives. During the subsequent hearing no explanations were found as to why Lieutenant Cripps opened out the engines to full power, which made the airship climb.

Two Zero Class airships at RNAS Pembroke – SS-Z16 and 17 – were the first to arrive at the station. (Courtesy of FAAM)

SSZ-37 being manhandled by ground crew. Note the station building in the background. (Courtesy B. Turpin)

SSZ-17 was the first of the class to be based at RNAS Pembroke. It was transported by road and assembled at the station on 7 August 1917. After the initial trials and familiarisation, it began flying convoy and anti-submarine patrols. Between August and December the airship flew 448 hours, and another fifty-three hours in three days in January 1918. However, Z-17 was destroyed in a shed fire on 3 January, which also destroyed part of one of the airship sheds. SSZ-16 was another airship transported to Milton and assembled and first flown from the station on 19 August 1917. The airship accumulated staggering flying hours for it flew a total 1,403 hours from August 1917 to November 1918. Most of the patrols were monotonous, without any sightings, and usually boredom crept in, and on a number of occasions caused crews to take risks. One of these occasions was on 7 December 1917 when SSZ-16 took off from Milton on a routine patrol in the Irish Sea. The airship was captained by Flight Lieutenant John E. Barrs. On her return flight to the base at 15.55, a submarine was spotted on the surface about a mile away. Barrs turned the airship towards the sighting, gaining height as he drew closer. While he identified the submarine as hostile, the U-boat's deck guns opened fire on the airship. His wireless operator F. E. Tattersall returned fire with his .303-inch Lewis gun, which strafed the deck and made the crew dive for cover. By the time the airship was over the submarine it had submerged. John Barrs dropped two 65-lb bombs, which had 2½-second delay fuses. The first bomb exploded some 25 feet off the port bow but the second failed to detonate. The engineer, J. W. Trevelyn, dropped a flare to mark the spot the submarine had been attacked. Upon his return to base two destroyers were observed going to the location. He sent information about the engagement ashore by an Aldis lamp as the airship's wireless was damaged. Flight Lieutenant John E. Barrs received the Distinguished Service Cross for the action.

In 1917, U-boat losses around the coast of north Wales were very few: three were sunk in the North Channel between southern Scotland and Ireland, especially in the Isle of Man area, and four in St George's Channel.

Two Zero types arrived at Llangefni on 13 March 1918, SSZ-50 and 51, both from Kingsnorth. While involved with night landing exercises at Malahide on 1 April SSZ-10's envelope ripped. The airship was repaired and returned to Llangefni.

More Zero Class airships were dispatched to RNAS Pembroke in the first part of 1918, such as SSZ-53 on 21 March 1918, which completed a total of 917 hours between then and its last flight in December 1918.

From the beginning of 1918, weather conditions around the Pembrokeshire coast had been dreadful. Spring brought better, clearer conditions and in March airship patrols covered 8,600 miles. Better conditions also gave an opportunity for night operation as U-boat activity had increased in the mouth of the Haven, preying on ships leaving Milford Haven. During April, airships and aircraft escorted eight outward convoys from Milford.

The next Zero type to be based at Llangefni was SSZ-34, which arrived on 23 March 1918 from Howden. It remained at Anglesey until being deflated and struck off charge on 26 November 1918, during which period it flew 859 hours on convoy duties.

With the formation of the Royal Air Force on 1 April 1918, all land-based air operations were handed over to the new force; as expected, RNAS Llangefni and Pembroke were transferred and became the responsibility of the RAF. Initially there were no changes

SSZ-17 at RNAS Pembroke. (Via FAAM)

whatsoever; the bases were still run by naval personnel and the aircraft and airships still kept their original markings.

SS Zero-37, built at Wormwood Scrubs, arrived at RNAS Pembroke on 2 April 1918. SSZ-56 followed on 18 April 1918, which arrived from Howden, but returned again to Howden in November.

Llangefni's first SS Zero patrol took place on 18 April 1918 by Z-35 under the command of Capt. T. B. Williams, but after some seven hours patrolling the Liverpool Bay area, they suffered an engine failure. The crew had no choice other than to make an emergency landing. Fortunately the airship came down near a fishing boat, which eventually towed it to safety so it could be beached at Llandudno where it was temporarily repaired and flown out to Llangefni for extensive repairs.

The first contact with a U-boat made by Llangefni's airships was on 18 May 1918, when SSZ-50 operating out of RNAS Anglesey located some oil slick in the sea near the Skerries, off the coast of Anglesey. The airship dived to 300 feet, dropping two 110-lb bombs. The contact was reported to other airships in the area, which relayed the message to patrolling warships. The destroyer *Do1* was first on the scene, dropping a depth charge pattern in the reported area, but no possible sinking could be verified. The search was continued early the following day by three airships from Llangefni. Some 12 miles off Bardsey Island, SSZ-51 located a wake of a periscope and recognised the dark shape of a submarine below the surface. As the airship reported the sighting to other craft it

Pembroke-based SSZ-37 flying low over the South Downs during trials.

dived, dropping its bombs on the target. SSZ-35 also joined in the attack but no hits were observed – one British and three American destroyers arrived at the scene, dropping their depth charges in a wide pattern. Soon debris and a large amount of oil rushed to the surface. After the war, records showed that U-boat *UB-119* perished under the Irish Sea, with its crew of thirty-four seamen, on that particular date.

To cope with large volume of work, RNAS Pembroke received another Zero craft (SSZ-67), on 22 May 1918, which flew to Milton from Kingsnorth.

On 27 May 1918, an enemy submarine was sighted some 5 miles off Pontllyfni, Gwynedd. Three Llangefni-based airships and two Royal Navy destroyers were dispatched to the area in Caernarfon Bay to make a search. Airship SSZ-34 dropped a 230-lb bomb on some sea disturbance in the vicinity, followed by SSZ-51 which, working in conjunction with a destroyer, dropped depth charges on suspicious bubbles on the surface. A submarine presence in the area was unlikely, and sea disturbances were often mistaken for submerged vessels. After the war, no records could be traced of enemy submarine activity in the particular area.

On 28/29 June, one of the longest endurance patrol flights ever recorded by any flying device at the time was made by SSZ-35 with Capt. Williams as pilot, with Flight Lieutenant Farina and Air Mechanic Rawlins as his crew. The twenty-six-hour and 15-minute patrol flight took them to Northern Ireland, across to Scotland, south to the

Isle of Man and across to Blackpool, where they were observed from the promenade. The final leg of the flight was to Liverpool and back to Llangefni, following the north Welsh coast. As they crossed the Anglesey coast, Lieutenant Farina decided to drop a bomb on rocks protruding out of the sea. Unfortunately, the airship was flying too low and a splinter from the exploding bomb punctured the envelope. Fortunately, Captain Williams managed to nurse the airship back to base. The majority of the patrols occurred in the Liverpool Bay area, escorting troopships into Liverpool and Manchester.

Perhaps the largest cargo vessel to be sunk off the Welsh coast was SS *Ethelina*, a 13,257-ton ship bringing iron ore from Spain to Barrow-in-Furness. The vessel was sunk by *U-103* some 15 miles north-west of the Skerries.

Between January and November 1918, a total of eighteen ships were sunk around the coast. With the introduction of twin-engine aircraft such as the Blackburn Kangaroo, Handley Page HP0/100, the Vickers Vimy and the twin-engine Felixstowe F2A flying boats, which had reasonable endurance, aircraft could now reach an area faster than an airship. In many circles it was felt that the age of the airship had come to an end, but there was still support in certain quarters determined to prove the viability of such craft. One such effort was achieving the endurance record; so on 29 June 1918, SSZ-35 broke the record once again. It flew north from Anglesey, across Scotland, down towards the Isle of Man, then eastward towards Blackpool and Liverpool, returning via the north Welsh

SSZ-37 was stationed at RNAS Pembroke April 1918–January 1919. (IWM)

SSZ-37 on an exercise with a warship in the Bristol Channel. (IWM)

coast to Holyhead, across Caernarfon Bay, down Cardigan Bay and the west coast of Wales before finally returning to Llangefni twenty-four hours later.

During a patrol on 11 August, SSZ-37 from Milton made a forced landing near Mumbles; the crew of three were rescued uninjured. The airship was picked up by a Swansea-based Royal Navy patrol boat and returned to Milton for repairs. On 18 November 1918, SSZ-37 was involved in towing trials with the naval vessel *PL.61* in the Bristol Channel. The airship continued to look for mines after the Armistice until it was deflated on 29 January 1919. Total hours flown were 675 hours 30 minutes.

After initial crew training, SSZ-51 took part in convoy patrol in Liverpool Bay and the Irish Sea. During one such flight on 2 April, the propeller tore the envelope while landing, which was a common occurrence with the Zeros. Three days later, the airship was forced to make an emergency landing at Iselo because of a ripped envelope. SSZ-51's final patrol from Plangent was on 15 September 1918; after suffering a deflation it had to be ditched at sea but the crew was rescued by an American warship, USS *Downs*.

Further attacks followed, such as on May 27 when SSZ-34 dropped a 230-lb bomb on a suspicious target, with no confirmation. SSZ-51 dropped bombs on some bubbles appearing in the water, again with no confirmation.

In June 1918, Milton-based airships escorted three liners loaded with American troops bound for France.

After a long patrol on 28 July 1918, SSZ-67 landed heavily at Pembroke, causing the envelope to be torn by the propeller. The airship was repaired and was later involved with the cover for American troopship convoys. The airship's last flight took place in December after flying a total of 639 hours.

A close-up of SSZ-28 taking off from Milton.

Llangefni-based SSZ-50 was damaged yet again in a gale at the base on 4 October, and while on a patrol on 18 November it was forced to land at Aberaeron.

On 10 October, the final sinking in the Irish Sea took place when the City of Dublin Steam Packet Company's morning mail boat RMS *Leinster* was sunk off the Kish Bank by the German submarine *UB-123* with a loss of 501 lives. That particular day's bad weather and gusty winds prevented any airships from taking off from Llangefni, which might have deterred *UB-123* from attacking the *Leinster*.

SSZ-35, another of the Llangefni-based airships, was lost at sea some 15 miles north-west of Holyhead on 17 October 1918 owing to a torn envelope.

SSZ-42 was based at Mullion but after a forced landing at Ilford Cammo, near Christchurch, it required a new envelope and modifications. On 17 June 1918 was despatched to RNAS Pembroke in November 1918 as SSZ-42A.

Another Zero type to be based at Pembroke was SSZ-46. Initially, it was meant to go to Folkestone but was sent to Milton to cover the American troopships coming from the States. During one patrol, SSZ-46 was fired on by an escorting warship, and was reported at the time as mistaken for a Zeppelin. The airship flew a total of 648 hours, the last flight taking place in November 1918.

There is no record of any airship sinking a submarine; several from Llangefni on Anglesey and Milton in Pembrokeshire were involved in various sightings and assisting surface ships to the scene. However, the airships' presence during escorting duties and patrolling proved more of a deterrent than actual threat. Most of the sinkings occurred when ships sailed

Inflating SSZ-53 inside Pembroke's large airship shed. (Courtesy of FAAM)

alone with no escort whatsoever. Perhaps the airship's greatest enemy was the weather, together with serviceability, which caused most of the accidents and fatalities. The airships based in Wales were rather fortunate to be well outside the range of German seaplanes, which were shooting down several aircraft on the south and south-east coasts of Britain.

Two airships inside the airship shed at Pembroke, SS-15 being repaired next to a Coastal. (Courtesy FAAM)

With the war coming to an end and land-based aircraft becoming more advanced and more capable of longer distances, it was felt in some quarters that the airship era was coming to an end. So there was an all-out effort to prove that the dirigible was still an effective weapon. On 21 October 1918, all U-boats were recalled to their bases, ending a grueling submarine campaign around the coast of Wales.

When the Armistice came on 11 November, there was great joy at both Llangefni and Pembroke bases. This notwithstanding, the airships continued to patrol for the rest of the year and for most of 1919, especially on mine patrols.

On 21 November 1918, SSZ-53 was patrolling an area in the Bristol Channel between the Gower Peninsula and Ilfracombe when it spotted three mines floating on the surface. The airship's Lewis machine gun was unable to explode the mines, therefore the location was sent to the mine sweeper based at Swansea. However, by the time the sweeper arrived, two of the mines had collided and exploded, leaving the third to be dealt by the Royal Navy.

Thousands of both enemy and Allied mines had been laid around the coast of the United Kingdom. Most had broken away from their anchorages and drifted into the sea lanes. A trawler operating out of Milford Haven was struck by a floating mine in January 1919. Once a mine was located, the airships would fire at it with two .303-inch Lewis machine guns to explode it. In one week Milton Zero airships destroyed at least twenty-three mines in St George's Channel and Carmarthen Bay.

The shadow of an airship flying over Carew village. (Courtesy of E. Perkins)

Part of the Armistice celebrations was a flight of an airship under the Menai Suspension Bridge. As it turned out to be during one of the victory parties, Major Probyn, who had given Captain Gordon Campbell a flight in one of the DH.6s under the Menai Bridge, challenged Major Elmhurst to do the same in an airship. Not to shy away from a challenge, Elmhurst, Campbell and Air Mechanic Charles Jones flew an SS Zero airship smoothly and without any problems under the bridge.

Most of the airships based in Anglesey and Pembroke were deflated between January and March 1919 and were shipped by road to RAF supply depots.

The following airships were stationed at RNAS Anglesey (Llangefni) and RNAS Pembroke (Milton).

RNAS Anglesey
Sea Scout SS-18, SS-22, SS-24, SS-25.
Sea Scout Pusher SSP-1, SSP-6, SSP-5.
Sea Scout Zero SSZ-31, SSZ-33, SSZ-34, SSZ-35, SSZ-50, SSZ-51, SSZ-72, SSZ-73.

RNAS Pembroke
Sea Scout SS-15, SS-37, SS-42.
Coastal Type C-3, C-6, C5-A.
Sea Scout Zero SSZ-16, SSZ-17, SSZ-28, SSZ-36, SSZ-37, SSZ-42A, SSZ-46, SSZ-52, SSZ-53, SSZ-56, SSZ-67, SSZ-76.

Chapter 4

Land-Based Aircraft Contribution

As the First World War progressed, Allied shipping losses were on the increase. The airship patrols and ships of the anti-submarine flotilla provided reasonable cover in the channels and approaches to the United Kingdom, but there was a blind area nearer the coastline known as the inshore area. U-boats of that era had a limited amount of time they could stay submerged, therefore they had to surface to recharge the batteries that powered the submarine electrical motors and enable the crew to breath fresh air. During this period, the submarine was very vulnerable to attack from the air. The inshore area became one of the favourite killing grounds for the U-boats as coastal shipping tended to sail close to the shore without any air or sea escort whatsoever.

Initially, this Airco DH.4 was sent to RNAS Anglesey.

In 1915, the Admiralty was faced with the ever-growing problem of enemy submarine activities around the British coastline. Several ships had been attacked and sunk; pressure was put on the Admiralty to combat the submarine threat and keep the sea-lanes safe. Therefore, all-out efforts were put in action to develop land bases for airships and land-based aircraft. However, priority was given to the airship bases, which were thought to be more suitable for the task because of their longer endurance.

It was not until 1917 that the U-boat threat to coastal shipping was realised in full. Admiralty maps plotting U-boat activities and sinkings showed that since the introduction of the convoy system and airship patrols, the enemy had changed their tactics and the majority of merchant ship losses were within 10 miles of land. The heaviest losses were on the north-east coast, the south-west and around the coast of Wales.

During December 1917, enemy submarines off the coast of Anglesey sank nine vessels of various tonnages.

The situation was not better around the south Wales coastline; colliers leaving the coal ports of Barry, Llanelli and Cardiff became prime targets for the German U-boat.

Aircraft of the period had very limited range and payloads and reliability was poor; they were not suitable for long-range patrols but were ideal for inshore duties and U-boat spotting. As the result of an Admiralty inquiry and pressure from the government, a series of seaplane stations and airstrips were built in prominent locations in the United Kingdom to supplement the airship stations that already existed. The bases were manned by RNAS personnel and equipped with aircraft withdrawn from the front-line squadrons. At the time, Royal Naval Air Service modern equipment was limited as all new aircraft entering service were required on the Western Front. However, in 1917 the Airco DH.4 and the Sopwith 1½ Strutter had been replaced and withdrawn for secondary duties in the United Kingdom.

A DH.4 outside a Bessoneau hangar.

Sopwith 1½ Strutter. Single-seat versions served with the RNAS at Milton.

It was reasoned that if coastal shipping lanes were patrolled regularly by aircraft at about 20-minute intervals, that would be enough to deter U-boats from attacking; these were called 'scarecrow patrols'. First choices of aircraft were the Sopwith 1½ Strutter and the Airco DH.4 bomber, which was thought highly of on the Western Front. Initially, a few of the type were issued to these Special Duties Flights but the aircraft eventually allocated was the Airco DH.6, which had been withdrawn from the front line for training. Even in its training roll it had been superseded by the Avro 504. RNAS had at least 300 DH.6s on their books and most had become surplus to their training requirements.

On 29 April 1917, the first aircraft to arrive at Milton were six Sopwith 9400 twin-seat and 9700 single-seat biplanes, or as the aircraft was better known, the Sopwith 1½ Strutter. These were naval bombers fitted with the RNAS Equal Distance Bomb Sight, which was regarded as the most sophisticated and most modern of all bomb-aiming equipment at the time. These Sopwith fighter-bombers got their name from an unusual arrangement of short and long pairs of centre-section struts. The aircraft was powered by a single 110 hp Clerget engine, which gave it a speed of 108 mph. It was armed with one Vickers machine gun and a Lewis machine gun, as well as four 25-lb bombs.

Initially seven aircraft were destined for RNAS Pembroke, but during transit one aircraft was severely damaged when it made an emergency landing en route to RNAS Pembroke. Further 1½ Strutters arrived at the base in June.

The Sopwith 1½ Strutters patrolled an area between the shoreline and up to over 100 miles offshore, while airships patrolled areas beyond the aircraft's range and endurance. The patrol area covered by the Pembroke-based flight was the entrance to Milford Haven, the south coast of Pembrokeshire, Carmarthen Bay and the Gower Peninsula. North of the county, including the sea lane between Ireland and Goodwick, was covered by the seaplanes based at Fishguard. As with the seaplanes, most of the patrols involved hours of monotonous flights over the sea, searching for enemy submarines or occasionally escorting coastal shipping from the ports of Llanelli and Swansea around the Pembrokeshire headland.

The first 1½ Strutter patrol flight took place on 29 April 1917 with Flight Sub-Lieutenant William Allaway at the controls. The flight lasted one hour and 10 minutes, covering an area from St Govan's Head to Pendine Sands.

On 12 July 1917, two 1½ Strutters were on patrol in an area some 75 miles south of Caldey Island when one of the aircraft spotted what seem to be a periscope wake on the sea surface. At once the aircraft dived, dropping two 100-lb bombs on the surface disturbance. Both aircraft circled the spot and an oil slick was observed on the surface. The second aircraft instantly dropped two 100-lb bombs on the slick, observing two large explosions. Unable to stay as their fuel was running low, they returned to Milton. Later that day an airship was returning to base after a patrol over the area but could not see any debris or oil slick.

On 4 August 1917, the flight suffered its first casualty when Flight Sub-Lieutenant Allaway failed to return from a long patrol in Carmarthen Bay.

The 1½ Strutters' flights were mostly single-manned as they were able to carry more fuel and bomb load.

The Admiralty came to the conclusion that both airships and land-based aircraft could work together, operating from the same base as they did at Milton. This arrangement was also intended for RNAS Anglesey, but after some trials and surveying the terrain it was found that the ground was too rough and needed extensive levelling, which would be too costly.

A Sopwith 1½ Strutter with a Scarffe gun mounting (two-seat version).

It was decided to send DH.4s to Anglesey, but their introduction was not as successful as the Sopwiths in Pembroke.

On 7 November 1917, six Airco DH.4 fighter-bombers from Castle Bromwich in the Midlands were sent to join the airships at Llangefni to provide inshore patrols. However, things did not go according to plan; due to bad weather, only two aircraft reached north Wales. One landed on Traeth Lavan near the village of Abergwyngregyn, but the aircraft was lost to the incoming tide, despite great efforts made by the crew and local farmers to retrieve the stricken aircraft bogged down in the wet sand on the beach. After a few days the engine, a Rolls-Royce Eagle, was salvaged and the fuselage was set on fire.

The other DH.4 (A7654), piloted by Second Lieutenant Bernard Carter, DSO, crashed within sight of the base at Llangefni. Unfortunately the pilot was killed and his observer, Corporal Harold Smith, was badly injured. The other aircraft completely lost their way to north Wales and decided to return to their base in the Midlands. Clearly, the introduction of land-based aircraft to Llangefni was a disaster because it had not been planned properly.

Long patrols often affected the pilots' navigation, such as in November 1917 when a Sopwith 1½ Strutter (believed to be A5277) escorting two trawlers back to Milford Haven reported spotting an object on the horizon and was going to investigate. The Strutter never returned to Milton and was believed to have crashed.

It was not until 1918 that a suitable landing strip for the land-based aircraft was found and built in north Wales. The landing site was situated in a coastal area between Bangor and the village of Abergwyngregin on the edge of the Snowdonia range. Fifty acres of land, which consisted of most of Glan y Mor Isaf Farm, were requisitioned in May 1918. Most of the airfields during the First World War were very basic and easy to construct.

Milton, on the other hand, was more developed with wooden huts, administration blocks, sick quarters and a technical section already in place at the airship station; only three Bessoneau hangars and additional accommodation huts were built to accommodate the Sopwiths.

After the formation of the Royal Air Force on 1 April 1918, the Special Duties Flights/coastal patrol flights were rearranged into six wings, with an HQ wing. On 8 August 1918, Wales came under 77 Wing, 14 (Marine Operational) Group, with its headquarters at Haverfordwest and the Special Duties Flight's headquarters at nearby Milford Haven. RNAS Pembroke kept its two flights, Nos 519 (A Flight) and 520 (B Flight) of No. 255 Squadron. There were two seaplane flights, 426 and 427 of No. 245 Squadron at Fishguard Bay. Nos 521 and 523 Special Duties Flights were transferred from Llangefni to Aber (Bangor) to become Nos 521, 522 and 530 Flights of No. 244 Squadron. A minor move was made just before hostilities ceased on 18 October 1918 when five Airco DH.6s of No. 530 Flight moved to Tallaght in Ireland. Even after the formation of the Royal Air Force on 1 April 1918, Nos 244 and 255 Squadrons kept their separate identities and their Royal Naval Air Service background.

The aircraft allocated for Special Duties Flights were Airco DH.6s, perhaps not the best choice for the task, but they were available in large numbers.

On 1 June 1918, fishing trawlers operating out of Milford Haven reported a sea disturbance some 150 miles south-west of the county. Two DH.6s (F3357 and unknown

A two-seat Sopwith 1½ Strutter landing at Milton.

serial number) from No. 518 Flight went to investigate. They were joined by SSZ-53 from RNAS Pembroke. Due to the DH.6s running low on fuel the aircraft returned to base, leaving the airship to continue the search. After intensive search nothing was seen and the airship continued its normal patrol.

Between 15 August and 23 November 1918, No. 244 Squadron's three flights received twenty-four Airco DH6 aircraft, six to replace those that had already crashed. Also in August 1918, RNAS Pembroke received ten Airco DH.6s from naval reserve stocks to supplement the 1½ Strutters already on charge. A further three reserve aircraft were added to the squadron inventory before the Armistice. These bombers were much slower than the Sopwiths but had a longer range and were more adaptable to patrol work.

No. 255 Squadron's first engagement against an enemy submarine was on 14 August 1918 when Lieutenant Arthur J. D. Peebles, flying DH.6 C9439, spotted a U-boat periscope. He attacked the target at 09.35 with a 100-lb bomb, witnessing air bubbles and an oil slick on the sea surface afterwards. His aircraft was not equipped with a radio so he could not report the sighting but returned to the base. At 12.20 Lieutenant Peebles and Captain Soar returned to the site for another attack. The Admiralty classed the attack as a possible damage.

On 14 August 1918, No. 244 Squadron lost two DH.6 aircraft flying from Llangefni prior to their move to Glan-y-Mor Isaf; C2021 failed to return from a patrol and DH.4 B3021, flown by Lieutenant J. R. Johnstone, who was killed when he suffered an engine failure while landing and crashed into a neighbouring field.

This Airco DH.6 was similar to the type flown by both Nos 244 and 255 Squadrons. (ADF Gallery)

This DH.6 was to become No. 244 Squadron's principle aircraft.

Throughout August the squadron was regularly patrolling the coastal sea lane extending from Anglesey to Liverpool Bay, usually taking over the patrol from the airships. On one such patrol, a ship reported a strange sea swell some 5 miles off the Great Orme, thought at the time to be a submarine submerging. Two DH.6s were sent to investigate and observed what was interpreted as a periscope wake. One of the aircraft dropped two bombs on the disturbance, but no sign of a U-boat.

The coastal patrol flights operated under a great deal of pressure and difficulty. The flights were constantly over-worked, frequently flying on one-hour patrols. The units were never up to strength in either aircrew or mechanics, most of whom were classed as unfit for active service in France, but were nevertheless extremely courageous with some even dying in action. On the Home Front there was a constant shortage of armourers, so bomb loading was usually done by mechanics and general personnel, which resulted in bombs not being primed and the machine guns jamming more frequently than usual. Often Nos 519 and 520 flights at Pembroke used the armourers from the airship station.

On 23 August 1918, DH.4 F3350 crashed in the sea during a combined patrol flying from Bangor with an airship from Llangefni; luckily for the crew the airship was able give directions to a rescue vessel from Menai Strait.

On 7 September 1918, No. 244 Squadron suffered its first fatal accident at the base when a DH.6 (B3023) crashed just after taking off. The pilot, Captain Tuck, and his observer, air mechanic W. Shaw, were badly injured and taken to Bangor hospital where W. Shaw later died from his injuries. The squadron lost another aircraft on 11 October when C2074 crashed in Caernarfon Bay; both crew were lost.

As there is no surviving airfield log, it is very difficult to obtain much information about the base. It would appear that the squadron was involved in several coastal patrols, going to the assistance of merchantmen in the area number of occasions, but there are no records of any of the aircraft involved with enemy submarines. However, it seems

A DH.6, belonging to No. 255 Squadron, taking off. (RNAS archives)

that one patrol went to the assistance of an airship from Llangefni that had mechanical problems and was in difficulty.

The squadron's greatest difficulty at Glan y Mor Isaf Farm was serviceability, for there was a shortage of trained mechanics and spare parts. From a peak in October 1918, the squadron had seventeen aircraft serviceable, but the numbers dropped within weeks to twelve and at one stage, only two. Fortunately, as spares gradually became available the figure was up again to a reasonable level by December, but by now there were a shortage of pilots as some had left to join other squadrons. The unit usually had twice as many aircraft as pilots to fly them.

The airfield itself caused a great many problems, especially during the winter months. As the result of a wet winter with heavy rain and strong winds, flooding occurred regularly, which made the base uncomfortable and even unbearable for personnel who were accommodated in tents. For most of the time during the winter months, the airstrip was water-logged and unserviceable. On a number of occasions aircraft became bogged down in the mud. At one point the base was declared non-operational, which caused a stir in the Admiralty.

Serviceability at RNAS Pembroke was rather better, as at any time the squadron could provide at least nine serviceable aircraft for patrol.

However, after the Armistice on 11 November 1918, Special Duties Flights' importance declined. For the next five weeks the flights were involved in mine searching along the coasts of Wales. Several mines, both British and the enemy's, had broken away from their

Sopwith 1½ Strutters served with distinction with RNAS at Milton.

moorings in rough seas and were drifting dangerously in the coastal sea lanes. Official records for No. 255 Squadron recorded nil patrols for the week ending 30 November 1918, but according to local newspapers the squadron's aircraft were seen flying after that date. However, No. 244 Squadron's aircraft were dispatched to an acceptance park in December and the squadron was officially disbanded on 22 February 1919.

In November 1918, Airco DH.6 aircraft on charge to Nos 244 and 255 Squadrons were as follows:

No. 255 Squadron Nos 519/520 Flights. (B2781, B2786, B2789, C2067, C2076, C9415, C9523, F3351, F3353, F3357.)
No. 244 Squadron Nos 521/522 Flights. (B2791, B2976, B2979, B3020, B3023, B3025, C6560, C6655, C6656, C7861, C7862, C7864.)
No. 530 Flight. (C6560, C7796, C7800, C7861, C7863.)

A month after the Armistice was signed, arrangements were in place for all anti-submarine flights and squadrons to be disbanded. The first to go were all the squadrons under No. 18 Group, with others following soon after.

In Wales the two squadrons of No. 14 Group were also disbanded; No. 255 at Pembroke on 14 January 1919 and No. 244 Squadron at Bangor on 22 February 1919. During the next few months, the canvas hangars, tented accommodation were removed. The personnel, stores and all equipment were removed by road to the railway station at Bangor. In May 1919, the land was released for farming and became Glan y Mor Isaf Farm once more.

The tactics adopted by the coastal patrol flights/Special Duties Flights were highly successful; during 1918 there were 4,869 sorties flown on escort duties by RAF aircraft and seaplanes from various bases around the United Kingdom. Only two vessels were actually attacked by submarines during the period. Bad weather was perhaps the biggest problem, preventing any flying, and the U-boats took advantage of the situation.

Chapter 5

The Seaplane Offensive

As the result of the mounting enemy submarine attacks on Allied shipping in the Irish Sea during 1917, Fishguard harbour became a Royal Naval Air Service seaplane base.

The first official inkling of establishing a base at Fishguard came in a letter by the vice-admiral commanding at Milford Haven to the *Pembrokeshire County Echo*, dated 4 March 1917, indicating that some personnel had already arrived at the site under the supervision of Squadron Commander J. T. Cull. However, it seems that naval personnel had already surveyed the area earlier to assess the bay's suitability for seaplane operations. Work on the new base was done by Messrs. Topham, Jones & Railton, the firm that was responsible for enlarging the harbour and building a new breakwater for Cunard and the Great Western Railway in 1909. No aircraft had been allocated to the base, but land was cleared and a canvas and wood hangar had been constructed. Over the next few months, a slipway and three adjoining brick buildings were built. A launching crane was installed on the new breakwater.

RNAS Fishguard, showing the slipway with a Sopwith Baby and Short 184 in front of hangars.

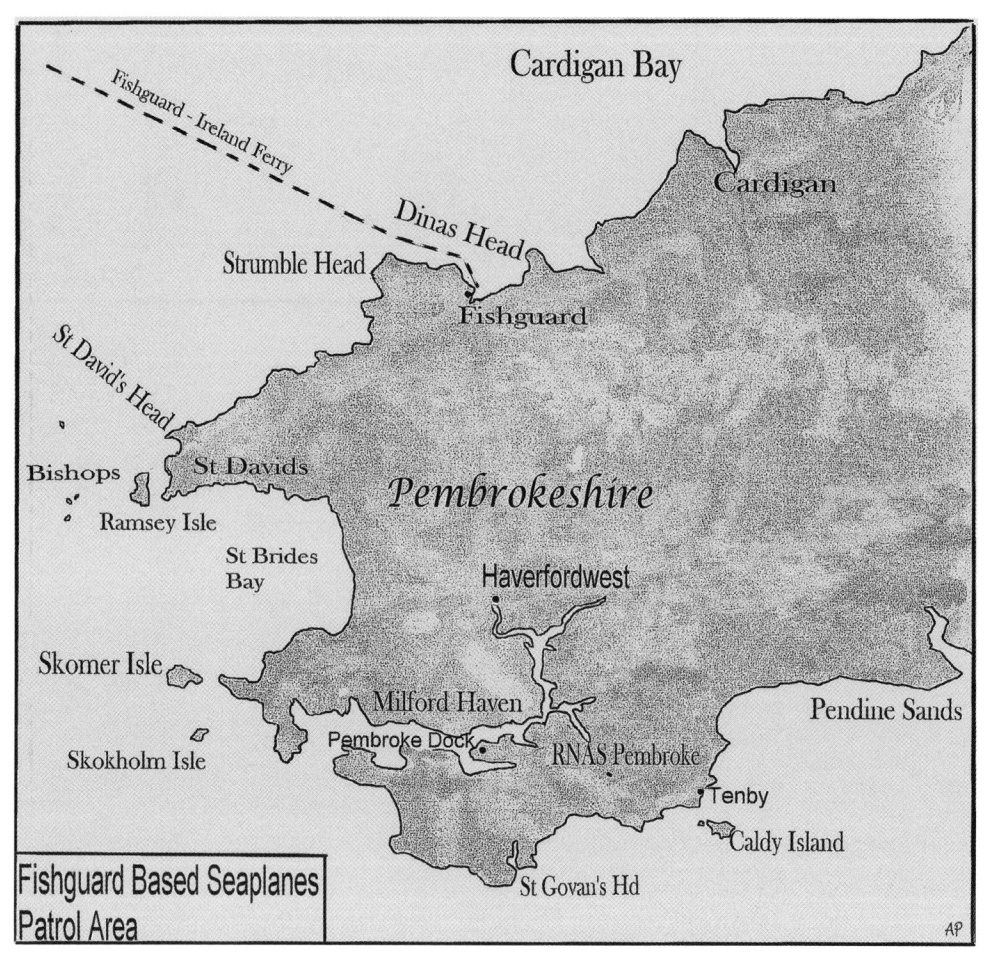

Map of RNAS Fishguard patrol area. (Alan Phillips Collection)

Over the years, attacks by enemy U-boats on coastal shipping had trebled. The submarines often used the rugged coastline of neutral southern Ireland for shelter. By the time a warship had reached the scene, the U-boat had disappeared, either to the open Atlantic or to the safety of the Irish coast. The only solution was to set up seaplane bases at strategic position along the coast.

Several areas in Wales were considered, such as the Menai Straits, the beaches at Rhyl in north Wales and Milford Haven and Burry Inlet in the south, but only Fishguard Harbour, with its sheltered bay, was finally chosen.

RNAS Fishguard was officially set up on St David's Day, 1 March 1917, by Squadron Commander John T. Cull, DSO, RN, of the Admiralty Air Department Special Service.

Initially, RNAS Fishguard came under the control of the Commander-in-Chief Plymouth. On 3 April 1917, the RNAS Seaplane Western Wing came under the authority of Wing Commander E. L. Gerrard; its headquarters were at Devonport and it oversaw the bases at Cattewater, Port Melon, Newlyn and Fishguard, as well as the airship stations at Mullion and Pembroke. In November 1917, Fishguard and

Pembroke became the South-West Group under the command of the senior naval officer based at Milford Haven.

The Admiralty's intention was to base two Royal Naval Air Service flights at Fishguard, consisting of six seaplanes – three Sopwith Babies or Fairey Hamble Babies and three Short Type 184 Seaplanes – but as the war progressed and the submarine threat became more intense, the number was doubled. All belonged to Nos 426 and 427 Coastal Patrol Flights of No. 245 Squadron with Major F. Denham Till as commanding officer.

The main types of seaplane operated from Fishguard by the RNAS and RAF were the Sopwith Baby, Fairey Hamble Baby and the Short 184.

The Sopwith Baby was the smallest of the seaplanes; the single-seater was powered by a 110 hp Clerget engine, which gave the aircraft a speed of 92 mph and an endurance of two hours in reasonable weather. It was armed with a single .303 Lewis machine gun and up to 130 lbs of bombs.

The Fairey Hamble Baby was a development of the Sopwith aircraft with the ailerons being replaced by a trailing edge flap enabling the aircraft to take off and land at lower speeds, therefore reducing strain on the engine. It was powered by the same Clerget engine, giving it similar speed and endurance to the original design.

The Short Type 184 was the largest of the Fishguard seaplanes. The two-seat aircraft was powered by a 220–240 hp Sunbeam Mohawk or Maori, or a Renault engine, which gave it a top speed of 88 mph and an endurance of nearly five hours. Its armament consisted of a .303 Lewis machine gun mounted on a Scarfe, or Whitehead mounting, in

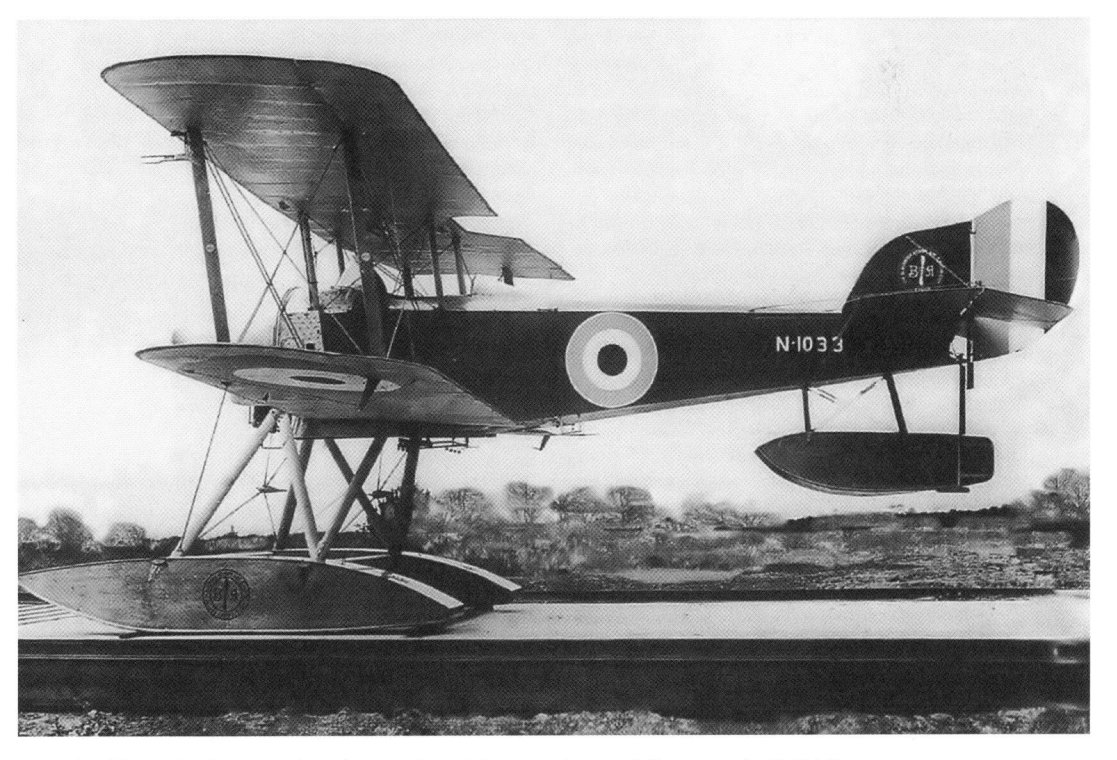

Blackburn-built Sopwith Baby seaplane N1033 prior to delivery to the RNAS.

Sopwith Baby being hoisted. (Courtesy of FAAM)

Fairey Hamble Baby (a modified version of the Sopwith design). (Via IWM)

the rear cockpit. The seaplane was designed to carry a 14-inch torpedo under the fuselage or up to 260 lbs of bombs.

The seaplane base consisted of one small hangar constructed of a wooden frame covered with canvas, which was used mostly for aircraft maintenance rather than storage as the seaplanes were usually moored in the bay. All accommodation was also under canvas, except the officers, who messed in the nearby Bay Hotel.

The first aircraft to arrive at Fishguard was a Blackburn-built Sopwith Baby (N1011) seaplane on 30 March 1917; within days, it began flying patrols in the vicinity, but mostly escorted ferries from Cork. The second Sopwith Baby (Blackburn-built N1033) arrived on 16 April 1917. Unfortunately, this aircraft, piloted by Flight Lieutenant R. E. Bush, crashed seven days later, before it flew its first sortie. Lieutenant Bush took off from the bay as normal but soon developed a power failure; he was unable to gain sufficient height to clear power lines from a nearby powerhouse which supplied the base. The aircraft swerved to avoid a building, struck a cliff face and burst into flames. Private B. Blackburn, of the King's Regiment based at Fishguard, was on sentry duty and managed to pull Lieutenant Bush from the burning aircraft, but tragically Flight Lieutenant Bush died from his injuries on 23 April. Although the flight was recorded in the station log as a test flight for the new engine, the aircraft carried two 16-lb bombs, which fortunately did not explode. According to a local newspaper, Lieutenant Bush had written to the local vicar requesting him to read out the banns of his forthcoming marriage. The funeral

A Sopwith Baby about to taxi away from the slipway. (Trevor Barnett Collection)

was conducted with full military honours: the cortège was escorted from Fishguard Bay Hotel to Goodwick railway station by RNAS personnel with men of the No. 3 Garrison Battalion; the King's Liverpool Regiment formed the guard of honour. Lieutenant Bush was buried at Keynsham Cemetery, Bristol.

Around this time, enemy submarine activity increased around the northern coast of Pembrokeshire, especially near the Fishguard–Rosslare ferry route. All aircraft were put on readiness and armed; when possible, a seaplane would take off just as a ferry sailed.

Both types of seaplanes were rather delicate aircraft – the slightest rough seas or gusty winds were enough to cause damage or flying accidents. On 24 April 1917, a Short 184 (9086) was damaged while taxiing in heavy seas, causing it to nosedive into the water; fortunately there were no casualties. Another Type 184 (N1149), piloted by Flight Sub-Lieutenant R. G. Clarke, crashed in bad weather into Windy Hill on 27 October 1917. According to the station log no casualties were recorded, but the aircraft was struck off charge on 2 November 1917. The incident was reported in the local *County Echo* newspaper.

One of the first recorded attacks on a U-boat was on 23 November 1917. Flight Sub-Lieutenant H. F. Delarue, piloting a Fairey Hamble Baby (N1199), was patrolling some 12 miles north-west of Strumble Head when he spotted a periscope wake at 1457 hours, heading in the direction of the Irish ferry. From a height of 1,000 feet, the pilot dived on the spot at full throttle, shutting off his engine at 500 feet and releasing his two 65-lb bombs. The engine was restarted and the seaplane returned to observe the result of the attack. One bomb failed to explode, but the second exploded about 10 feet of the disturbance. White bubbles and a large area of disturbed sediment appeared on the water, but there was no sign of what had seemed to be a periscope wake. Three other armed seaplanes were despatched from the base to the area, but nothing was sighted.

Also, in November 1917 two aircraft from Fishguard went to the aid of a trawler, which had been attacked by a surfaced U-boat. By the time the aircraft got to the scene, the submarine had gone and the trawler was limping back to port. However, on their return to Fishguard, one of the aircraft spotted what looked as a periscope trail in the sea. The Short 184 made a low pass and dropped two 25-lb bombs – at least one of the bombs exploded but they could not confirm a kill.

On 8 December 1917, another submarine contact was made by Flight Sub-Lieutenant W. G. Westcott and K. F. Alford in a Short 184 (N1683); two bombs were dropped on the wake but there was no possible confirmation of a kill.

During the First World War, radio communication between aircraft and bases was in its infancy. Carrier pigeons played a vital role in communicating between the seaplanes and shore base. The single-seat aircraft would land on the sea, providing it was calm, and release the pigeon with the message attached to its leg, while in the two-seat type, the pigeon would be released by the observer when the machine was in flight. At Fishguard, two airmen were responsible for the pigeons.

Patrolling over water in flimsy seaplanes of First World War vintage was extremely risky and dangerous, with several factors such as technical reliability, weather and pilot disorientation causing most accidents. One such accident happened on 21 February 1918 when Flight Sub-Lieutenant Cyril Gordon Duckworth, flying a Fairey Hamble Baby N1457, failed to return from a patrol in Cardigan Bay. The aircraft was last sighted

The pilot of a Sopwith Baby releasing a pigeon.

between Cardigan Head and New Quay, which was outside the safe patrol radius for a Hamble Baby. It seemed that Duckworth had run out of fuel and landed his seaplane in the sea. When the St Dogmaels lifeboat reached the reported position there was no sign of the wreckage or the pilot. The majority of the aircraft was eventually salvaged and the rest was washed up ashore later, but Sub-Lieutenant Duckworth's body was never recovered.

According to records, the seaplanes based at Fishguard made several sightings, but there is no record of any submarines being either damaged or sunk. However their presence was a deterrent, as on a few occasions surfaced submarines made a hasty retreat when a seaplane appeared on the horizon.

Another sighting occurred on 22 March 1918 when a Sopwith Baby (N1127) and a Short 184 (N1638) spotted the usual periscope wake in the sea while patrolling an area north-west of Fishguard. At once, the Sopwith manoeuvered into an attack position and dropped a single 65-lb bomb; a heavier 100-lb bomb was dropped by the Short 184. None of the pilots could confirm a kill, but the submarine was probably damaged. A Short 184 (N2765) was on what was classed as emergency patrol in the same area when the pilot observed a large disturbance and air bubbles coming to the surface of the water. The aircraft dived on the contact, dropping one 100-lb bomb; yet again no confirmation of a kill could be attained, but the disturbance ceased.

On 13 March 1918, Air Mechanic F. G. Hayward was flying as an observer in a Short 184 (N2843) when he spotted a surfaced U-boat north of Fishguard, but as the aircraft dived on the submarine, it received light machine-gun fire from the U-boat. No damage was inflicted on either the submarine or the seaplane. Air Mechanic Hayward was again in action on 20 April when Short 184 (N2765), piloted by Lieutenant E. S. Smith, dropped

Another of the seaplanes based at Fishguard was the Short 184 type.

Short 184 taking off in rough sea.

two 100-lb bombs on a submerged submarine positioned north-west of Dinas Head. One bomb failed to explode and yet again it was an inconclusive conformation.

Prior to August 1917, operational statistics for patrols flown by seaplanes from Fishguard were included in South-West Group statistics. It was only after that date that statistics were kept for the seaplane station itself. A typical example of operational statistics for March 1918 were as follows:

> Week ending 2 March – A total of five patrols were flown, one was a routine search, two were emergency patrols and two had to be aborted just after take-off because of cloud cover. Duration of the patrols was three hours and 28 minutes covering about 240 miles.
> Week ending 9 March – Eleven patrols were flown totaling ten hours 21 minutes and covering a total of 681 miles.
> Week ending 16 March – The weather improved considerably, enabling thirteen patrols to be made covering a distance of 1,418 miles and lasting over twenty-one hours.
> Week ending 23 March – The weather remained good, therefore nineteen patrols were flown during the week covering 2,199 miles and lasting thirty-three hours.
> Week ending 30 March – A total of eleven patrols to Bishops, Smalls, St Brides, Cardigan Bay and to Bardsey Island were made covering a distance of 1,473 miles and lasting twenty-one hours 58 minutes.

These were exceptionally good statistics for one month for the station, compared with the record for January 1918, when the unit only flew ten sorties covering only 839 miles and lasting twelve hours due to bad weather.

A Short 184 taking off from Fishguard Bay. (Via IWM)

With the forming of the Royal Air Force on 1 April 1918, RNAS and RFC came under one independent control. All RNAS assets and personnel were transferred to the new organisation. The station at Fishguard became part of the No. 14 Coastal Operation Group and the unit was formed into Nos 426 and 427 Flights under No. 77 Wing RAF on 20 May 1918. On 30 August the two flights were merged to become No. 245 Squadron RAF.

By April 1918, the squadron was standardised on the Short 184 seaplane, which was regarded as more suitable for long-range patrols and was capable of carrying a crew of two, which was essential for such missions.

During the first week in May another submarine was reported in the Cardigan Bay area and was attacked by a Short 184, again with inconclusive results.

Short 184 N2765 notched up considerable more flying hours than most of the seaplanes based at Fishguard but on 10 May, after a lengthy patrol, smashed its tail float in a forced landing in foggy conditions.

Also during May, Short 184 (N2796) was badly damaged and written off after a heavy landing in strong wind.

On 29 June a large patch of oil was spotted on the surface by an airship returning from a patrol. A Short 184 N2908 piloted by Lieutenant Carr was vectored to the position and dropped one 100-lb and one 280-lb bomb on the slick; again the attack was inconclusive.

Positive results were very rare, but on 6 July 1918 the squadron had a success when a Short Type 184 (N2830), crewed by Lieutenant E. A. Eames and Air Mechanic Hayward, spotted a sea disturbance in a north-western direction. The aircraft dived, dropping a 230-lb bomb on the position – within minutes, oil and air bubbles were observed rising to the surface, indicating the submarine had been damaged. After the war a U-boat was recorded as being damaged in the vicinity and had to make for port for repairs. Throughout the rest of the month and August there were five incidents of aircraft dropping bombs on oil patches and periscope wakes.

A Short 184 (N2830) being hoisted ashore.

On 10 July, two Short 184s, N2843 and N908, spotted an oil patch on the sea surface while patrolling Square 64Z. Both aircraft dropped their bombs but no result was observed.

During August, Fishguard's seaplanes recorded two incidents: one on 13 August when Short 184 (N2790) bombed another oil patch and on 16 August a periscope was sighted, but visual contact was lost and an attack did not occur.

What is believed to be the last recorded action involving Fishguard seaplanes took place on 3 September 1918 when Short Type 184 N2908 observed some oil slick and air bubbles off St David's Head. The seaplane dived, dropping two bombs on the suspected position; it remained in the area for 10 minutes but saw nothing else, eventually returning to base.

On 16 September 1918, SS *Serula*, a 1,388-ton cargo vessel, sent out an SOS that it had been struck by a torpedo. Two Short 184 seaplanes were dispatched from Fishguard to the scene but were unable to make any contact with a U-boat. However, it was able to direct a trawler and lifeboat to the scene to pick up survivors.

Most of the anti-submarine patrols undertaken by aircraft of No. 245 Squadron from Fishguard involved hours of monotonous searching for telltale signs, such as oil slick, surface sea disturbances, a periscope and its wake or even a surfaced submarine, which was a bonus. According to station log between a period of 15 June and 9 November 1918, No. 245 Squadron flew a total of 865 patrols lasting approximately 1,703 hours and covered some 39,522 miles from Milford Haven to the Llyn Peninsula. The busiest week was week ending 6 July 1918 when the Short 184 seaplanes flew twenty-four

Short 184 N1242 being prepared for flight. (Via FAAM)

Fishguard Bay Hotel was used by the officers.

anti-submarine patrols lasting over eighty-eight hours and covering a distance of 5,171 miles, mostly in the Cardigan Bay area. It was not until after the Armistice that the general public knew the splendid work done by the personnel based in such camps as Fishguard.

It was reported by HQ at Milford in May 1918 that they knew of the whereabouts of the airships patrolling the seas, as well as ships of the naval anti-submarine flotilla and twenty-three enemy submarines in their controlled area from reports gathered by aircraft from Fishguard and Milton. Most of the report was geared to uplift the population's morale that the U-boat menace had been overcome.

The local newspaper, *The County Echo*, often reported on the base, perhaps not fact but rather propaganda regarding the heroic patrols and even the sinking of imaginary submarines. The articles gave the local inhabitants a flavour of what action was like. The stories were often cleared by the censors because they were classed as a tonic to public morale.

The actual U-boat sinkings were far above the true figures.

After the war ended in 1918, the base was dismantled in early 1919 and its personnel and equipment were transferred to other bases, leaving no evidence whatsoever that a seaplane base ever existed. However, according to local residents, a few of the concrete moorings did exist for some time after, and were used by local fishermen to moor their boats. They too disappeared with redevelopment and the strengthening of the sea defences. At the time of writing only the concrete slipway remains.

Aircraft based at Fishguard between March 1917 and October 1918.

Blackburn-built Sopwith Baby and Fairey Hamble-built Baby

N1011, N1033, N1124, N1433.
N1199, N1205, N1457.

Short Type 184 Seaplane

9086, N1086, N1149, N1683, N1684, N1742, N1797, N2657, N2658, N2659, N2790, N2796, N2828, N2830, N2842, N2843, N2907, N2908, N2940, N2941, N2942, N9032, N9033.

Chapter 6

Flying Training in Wales During the First World War

The only site associated with flying training in Wales was at Shotwick/Queensferry, Flintshire.

The first idea of a flying school was initiated by Mr T. Murray Dutton in 1914, who obtained an area of grassland near the River Dee estuary. Initially known as Queensferry, Mr Dutton, an engineer and a keen aviator, began manufacturing the French-designed Caudron G3 biplane in his purposely built hangars, sheds and workshops there. The flying school began in 1916, equipped with two Caudrons and an Avro 521. Over the next few months several trainees went through the school before finishing their courses at Hendon.

Thomas Dutton pioneered training in Wales in 1916. He was based at Queensferry/Shotwick. Here, aircraft are undergoing maintenance in the hangar there. (Courtesy of Denbigh Archives)

Dutton's two Caudron biplanes at Queensferry. (Courtesy of Denbigh Archives)

Until 1917 most military pilots were trained in civilian schools that were run by aviators who had obtained their Royal Aero Club certificates. Several went as civilian instructors to Hendon, which became the main training base for the Royal Flying Corps.

It became a base for two RFC training squadrons, Nos 95 and 96, equipped with a variety of standard Royal Flying Corps aircraft of the time, namely Camels, Pups, Dolphins, Salamanders, Martinsyde and Avro 504s. Most of these types were still serving on the Western Front. Both squadrons arrived within days of each other: No. 95, from Ternhill, on 30 October 1917, and No. 96, from South Carlton, a few days later. Both squadrons remained at Shotwick until April 1918.

In November 1917, No. 90 Squadron arrived at Shotwick under the command of Major Blackwood with additional Avro 504s and Sopwith Dolphins. This caused problems at the airfield, so additional land was requisitioned and temporary hangarage had to be provided.

On the day that the Royal Air Force was formed, on 1 April 1918, another fighter squadron, No. 61 equipped with Camels, Pups, and an Avro 504, arrived from Shawbury.

The training policy was to train a complete squadron together, and after the training was completed the personnel would be sent to an active squadron on the Western Front or to other theatres of war.

While waiting posting to France in April, Nos 95 and 96 Squadrons were disbanded and the pilots and their aircraft were dispersed to other squadrons, home and overseas.

This system relieved the acute parking problems that accumulated at the airfield.

No. 90 Squadron's Sopwith Camels and Pups left Shotwick on 18 July 1918 for RAF Brockworth.

With the impending departure of the three fighter squadrons, the airfield was designated a training base. First arrivals on 1 April 1918 were No. 55 Squadron, from RAF Lilbourne, and No. 67 TS (Training Squadron), from RAF Shawbury equipped with

Camels, SE5s and Avro 504s. These two squadrons became the basis for No. 51 Training Depot Station on 15 July 1918.

By 1918, there was some standardisation in both pilots' and observers' training. No. 51 TDS was split into three units; the day-fighter training establishment had a compliment of thirty-six Avro 504s and thirty-six Sopwith Dolphins, which had become the standard trainers. Surprisingly, due to a shortage of suitable aircraft, a third flight was never formed. The formation of the training unit did not go smoothly and it had a worrying impact on the station and the local area when the aircraft began crashing. In six months at least seventeen such incidents took place, with nine pilots who were either killed instantly or later died from their injuries; they were buried in the local churchyard.

As was quite common with any training establishment, accidents were frequent. Mechanical faults or engine failures caused most of the accidents, but some were attributed to inexperienced pilots. One such accident happened on 27 January 1918 when 2nd Lieutenant John Brendel (a Canadian) piloted a Sopwith Pup B5792 and was killed when he had an engine failure at 6,000 feet and crashed into the Mersey. This was the first fatal accident recorded by No. 90 Squadron.

Others were fortunate to walk away with just minor injuries, such as 2nd Lieutenant A. L. Fachnie, who misjudged his landing and crashing when his Avro 504 developed an engine failure on his return to Shotwick. Lieutenant Fachnie was also unfortunate enough to be involved in another incident on 2 October 1918, when his Sopwith Camel E7297 crashed on landing; fortunately he only sustained minor injuries.

On 8 April 1918, Second Lieutenant B. S. Crecine of No. 90 Squadron received minor injuries when flying a Sopwith Dolphin, C4140, which experienced engine failure while taking off.

Another fatality occurred on 25 April 1918 when an Avro 504, C599, piloted by 2nd Lieutenant John Jewett Miller (USA) who was flying with No. 95 Squadron, crashed. On 27 April 1918, Sopwith Pup B1742, piloted by Lieutenant Victor William Lowrie (RAF), a flying instructor at Shotwick, hit an air pocket and spun in at low altitude. Unfortunately, he later died of shock and injuries.

Sopwith Camels were used for training but were difficult to control. (Courtesy of MAP)

Sergeant C. V. Simmonds of No. 67 TDS was seriously injured on 18 May 1918 when his Camel, C112, suffered an engine failure at 50 feet; as the result the aircraft stalled and landed heavily.

The Sopwith Camel was involved in more mishaps and accidents than any other type while serving with No. 51 TDS, the reason being the aircraft was not particular easy to fly, being extremely sensitive on the controls. Its forward-placed centre of gravity, which was due to the concentration of weight (pilot, engine, the fuel tank and armament), made it easy to spin to one side. However, in the hands of experienced pilots it was a formidable fighter and proved its worth over the Western Front, accumulating more 'kills' than any other Allied aircraft. Between August and the end of the year, nine Camels crashed during training sorties.

Four pilots tragically lost their lives and were buried locally; five were injured and hospitalised. Two Avro 504s and an SE5 also crashed on training flights.

On 2 August 1918, the aerodrome at Shotwick became known as North Shotwick, and Queensferry became known as South Shotwick – names that remained throughout the twenties.

By now the RAF had restructured its training programme, concentrating on the larger airfields. A new training syllabus was drawn up for the students and proper training aircraft were provided. However, the war came to an end before a fully integrated training programme could be instigated. Demand for fully trained pilots more or less ceased, but Shotwick continued to train pilots.

At the end of the war the Royal Air Force was the largest air force in the world; as soon as the Armistice was signed, plans were put in action to make a massive reduction in its size. Squadrons and their aircraft were returned from overseas bases to the UK for disbandment; therefore a number of squadrons and their aircraft returned to Shotwick for storage and disposal.

The Avro 504 became the standard training aircraft with the RFC.

Chapter 7

Welsh Air Bases During the First World War

Before 1914, several landing fields were established in the country by the early aviators and were used regularly for demonstration flights, such as Ely Aerodrome at Cardiff, Stradey Park at Llanelli, Rhos-on-Sea and Foryd Moor near Rhyl, but surprisingly none was considered suitable as a military airfield during the war. Admittedly, some of the sites were restricted and would restrict any further expansion and development.

The bases were as follows:

Abergwyngregin (RNAS Bangor)

The landing site was situated in a coastal strip between Bangor and the village of Abergwyngregin, on the edge of the Snowdonia range.

Fifty acres of land, which consisted mostly of Glan y Mor Isaf Farm, were requisitioned in May 1918 as the Llangefni airship station was found unsuitable for land-based aircraft.

Most of the airfields during the First World War were very basic and easy to construct. At Glan y Mor Isaf Farm hedges were removed to provide an enlarged area for landing and taking off, and Bessoneau hangars were constructed, usually on the grass. These hangars were the most common and easily constructed types at the time, consisting of a wooden frame covered with canvas. All accommodation, for officers and other ranks, was housed in various-sized tents. Stores, fuel and ammunition were stored in a separate site protected by sandbags and covered by tarpaulin in nearby woods away from the main site. Some farm buildings were confiscated for use as a wireless room and for briefing crews.

Dale, Pembrokeshire

This site was used for testing the hydroplanes Burney X2 and 3 in 1912. A small hangar was built as well as a concrete slipway near the village of Dale. Although the initial tests were disappointing, further trials occurred a year later with the first flight taking place in October 1913. The Admiralty cancelled the Burney project but continued with other seaplane designs. The Dale site was considered in 1916 as a seaplane base but rejected as it was felt that Milford Haven could be best utilised as a naval base.

RNAS Fishguard, Pembrokeshire

This seaplane base was situated north of the railway station and the furthest end of the quay, sheltered by the harbour breakwater.

The base consisted of one small hangar, constructed using a wooden frame covered with canvas, and three adjoining sheds, which was used mostly for aircraft maintenance rather than storage as the seaplanes were usually moored in the bay. All accommodation was also under canvas, except the officers who messed in luxury at nearby Fishguard Bay Hotel. Space for tented accommodation was limited; some ratings were accommodated in Goodwick village and in two railway carriages provided by the Great Western Railway.

Work on the new base was done by Messrs. Topham, Jones & Railton, the firm that was responsible for enlarging the harbour and building a new breakwater for Cunard and the Great Western Railway in 1909. No aircraft had been allocated to the base but land was cleared and a canvas and wood hangar had been constructed. Over the next few months a slipway and three adjoining brick buildings were built. A launching crane was installed on the new breakwater. Arrangements were made for the former GWR garage to be converted to store 1,000 gallons of fuel until a more permanent installation was built. An inventory check completed in April 1918 listed a dope shed, a small photographic hut, wireless hut, meteorological hut, and a compressor shed.

View of RNAS Fishguard's seaplane base, taken from a nearby hill.

A wooden hut surrounded by sandbags was used as magazine and detonator store, which was situated away from the slipway and hangars. A guardroom and a wooden gate guarded the entrance from the harbour. Medical facilities on the base were nonexistent, although arrangements were made with the contractors, using their small two-bed sick quarters. The nearest civil hospital was at Haverfordwest and the nearest military one at Pembroke Dock. A report published two days before the Armistice on 11 November 1918 as the result of an inspection in September criticised the lack of proper medical provisions at the base.

A 35-foot motor launch was provided by Pembroke Dockyard as a seaplane tender and rescue boat.

The Admiralty was always eager for its personnel to be involved in the community, but with strict instruction not to divulge any operational matters. The 'Fishplane', as the station team was known, entered all kind of sports events in the town. Several events were also held at the Bay Hotel, with local dignitaries invited.

The last recorded action took place on 3 September 1918, although few flights were done afterwards. By January 1919, most of the aircraft were dismantled and shipped out by train; only a few Short Type 184s remained. Demobilisation was gradual; the first to leave the base were the local WRNS in February 1919, and the rest left in early March. On 10 May the station was decommissioned and demolished.

Llangefni (RNAS Anglesey)

RNAS Anglesey is located between the A5 and B5109 roads, which had all-round clearance. Several sites in Anglesey were considered as a site for airship operations, but the Admiralty eventually acquired over 200 acres of farmland 3 miles from the town of Llangefni. In the four years the station was operational it had a variety of names, including Bodfordd and Gwalchmai – the nearest villages – Llangefni and Heneglwys. As the Welsh names caused problems in the Admiralty it was officially referred to as RNAS Anglesey. The air station consisted of one 'Coastal shed', which was a large 120 foot × 318 foot × 80 foot airship shed with large windshields on either end. These were permanent hangars with heavy steel frames covered in corrugated iron sheets. They were capable of storing two inflated Coastal-type and two SS-type airships side by side. Several wooden and corrugated huts were constructed as workshops and stores and a gas production unit was situated near the airship shed. The accommodation site, including administration and a w/t block, was situated near the A5 Holyhead to Menai Bridge main road. A Bessoneau hangar was added later to accommodate aircraft of the coastal patrol flight.

Initially the station complement was eighteen officers, twelve warrant officers and NCOs, twenty-seven corporals, 146 women Naval Air Service and sixteen civilian households' staff. The complement was increase in June 1918 with the arrival of the two coastal patrol flights but reverted back to its original staff in August. The commanding officers stayed at the Bull Hotel, Llangefni, and travelled daily to the station. The huts nearest the road were allocated to the NCOs and other ranks with the two officer quarters huts further back.

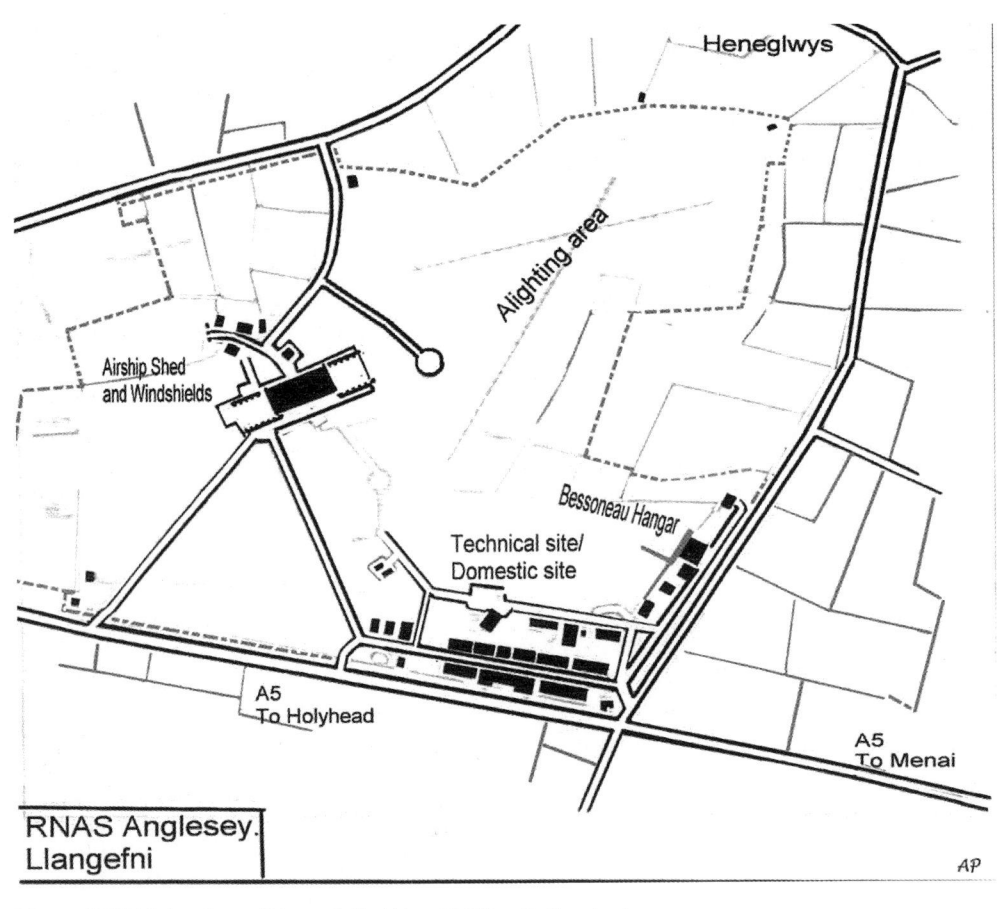

Map of RNAS Anglesey (Llangefni). (Alan Phillips Collection)

RNAS Anglesey officers' quarters in 1918. (Courtesy of Anglesey Archives)

Llangefni airship station (RNAS Anglesey) was commissioned on 26 September 1915 as part of No. 14 Group, which was responsible for the protection of the British coastline. The station's first commanding officer was Major George Scott, who eventually became Deputy Director of Airship Development, but tragically lost his life in the R101 crash in France in 1930.

He was the CO from September 1915 to October 1916 and was followed by Squadron Commander Corbett-Wilson from October to May 1917, then S/Cdr Brotherton until March 1918 and the last commander until closure was Major Thomas Elmhirst. The landing areas faced the two opening ends of the large shed. Two pairs of windshields extended out at each end towards the landing areas.

RNAS Anglesey was a base for Sea Scout (SS) type, Sea Scout Pusher (SSP) type and Sea Scout Zero type (SSZ) airships. On 6 June 1918, Nos 521 (A Flight) and 522 (B Flight) coastal patrol flights were formed at Llangefni and equipped with eight Airco DH4s (later replaced with DH6s). The flights were part of No. 255 Squadron RNAS until 15 August, when the unit moved to the new base at Aber (Bangor) where it was renumbered No. 244 Squadron. The Llangefni site was ideal for airships, but the ground was rather uneven for aircraft operations. The station closed in 1919 but the Admiralty did not relinquish the site until 1920, when it was passed onto the Government Disposal Board. The site was bought by Anglesey County Council and the domestic buildings were used as a small local hospital while others were being constructed in the area. By the end of the decade all the buildings, including the airship shed, were dismantled

RNAS Anglesey's hydrogen storage tanks. (Via R. Sloan)

and sold. During the Second World War the site was utilised again in 1942 as an RAF training airfield – RAF Mona.

Station's Commanding Officers:

September 1915–Oct 1916: Initially commanded by Major G. H. Scott.
October 1916–May 1917: Squadron Commander A. Corbett-Wilson.
May 1917–March 1918: Squadron Commander Brotherton.
March 1918–November 1918: Major Thomas Elmhirst.
November 1918–June 1919: Major Thomas Elmhirst.

Milton (RNAS Pembroke), Pembrokeshire

The base at Milton, which was often referred to by the same name, occupied some 228 acres near the village of Sageston, just off the main road between Pembroke and Carmarthen, but did not take shape until early January/February 1916. Initially the airship station had two 338 foot × 112 foot × 100 foot corrugated iron hangars with associated windshields, although one was seriously damaged in a fire in January 1917 and had to be completely dismantled. A smaller ex-army portable shed was considered but was never built. A result of the fire was that only three inflated machines could be stored; sheltered quarries were considered as suitable mooring – one at St Florence was recommended but not used.

RNAS Pembroke – main gate to the airship station and guardroom. (Via B. Turpin)

Although the dimensions of the sheds were standardised during 1915, the introduction of larger rigid airships by the Admiralty meant that larger hangars continued to be built in order to accommodate them. Most of the airship sheds were built by a little-known military unit, the Air Construction Corps.

Workshops, a power station and two lots of hydrogen storage tanks were constructed next to the hangars and the gas production units. Further wooden and canvas workshops, a sickbay, mess halls, wireless hut and both officers', NCOs' and other ranks' quarters were situated just off the main road. The accommodation consisted of a mixture of wooden and canvas huts. In 1918 station personnel included twenty officers, fifteen WO/NCOs, thirty corporals, and 189 women of the Naval Air Service who worked as W/T operators, clerks, drivers, riggers and mechanics. Also, there were thirty-one household staff (cleaners, cooks etc.). The station's complement increased by about sixty with the arrival of the Sopwith 1½ Strutters and later DH 6s. The entrance and the main gate to the station, with the guard room and main admin hut on either side, were just off the public road. The white painted wooden gate had a notice that read 'RN Airship Station Private'.

RNAS Pembroke was officially classed as fully operational in April 1916.

In 1917, three Bessoneau hangars, together with tented accommodation, were built in the south-east corner of the station on the Hazelbrook Farm side for the naval aircraft stationed on the base. The station's personnel establishment varied depending on the type of airships operated from 160–180, but increased to over 210 in 1917. The site operated the Sea Scout SS type, the large Coastal Class and the Sea Scout Zero SSZ type, which were actively involved in patrolling the sea lanes and the south-western approaches. On 29 April 1917, the airships were joined by aircraft from the Navy's special patrol flight, equipped with Sopwith 1½ Strutter bombers, and later by Airco DH.6s. The flight was part of No. 255 Squadron, which covered all of Wales. In 1918, the two flights Nos 519 and 520 amalgamated

RNAS Pembroke's airship hangar, a corrugated iron shed. The one at Anglesey was very similar. (Via D. Brock)

becoming No. 255 Squadron, and Flights 521, 522 and 530, based at Bangor, became No. 244 Squadron.

The seaplane base at Fishguard and RNAS Pembroke came under the command of No. 14 Group with its headquarters in Haverfordwest.

No. 255 Squadron was disbanded during February and March 1919. In 1920, the Admiralty relinquished the site and it was taken over by the Disposal Board in March for disposal and was eventually demolished. The land was sold at an auction in April 1923. Some ten years later the site was requisitioned as a site for an airfield with concrete runways to become RAF Carew Cheriton.

Shotwick and Queensferry (Sealand) Flintshire

Sealand airfield occupied two landing strips on either side of the main railway line connecting England to north Wales. As a consequence, two separate airfields were developed: Shotwick as a training station for the Royal Flying Corps and Queensferry as an aircraft acceptance park. The Queensferry site on the southern side was not developed as quickly as the Shotwick site and the war was over before it became fully operational.

The main site was the north camp (Shotwick), where most of the flying activities took place.

Bessoneau type were the standard hangars at Welsh bases.

It became the base for Nos 95 and 96, which were equipped with various RFC fighters including Sopwith Camels, Pups, Dolphins, Salamanders, Martinsydes and the Avro 504, which became the standard training aircraft with both RFC and RNAS. Pilots were trained on the aircraft they would fly operationally.

The Shotwick site was built on land reclaimed when the River Dee was diverted in 1737. At the outbreak of the First World War, the area was very rural and used for farming until engineer Mr T. Murray Dutton obtained an area of grassland and started a flying school. The school began in 1916 and he soon began building his own flying machines based on the French Caudron design in a purposely built hangar. Initially, most of the flying training done in the country was by privately owned civilian flying schools, which were eventually taken over by the RFC in 1917.

Dutton's flying school was located on the site which today is referred to as south camp and referred to locally as Queensferry air strip. It consisted of one long timber hangar capable of holding four aircraft with one door in the centre.

The War Office soon realised the potential of the site for training, therefore land on either side of the railway line was requisitioned. Work soon progressed on the sites, firstly on Shotwick aerodrome and later on Queensferry.

The entrance to the Shotwick site was halfway down the embankment and over the railway line. Wooden offices and living accommodation for 839 personnel, which included 209 women, was constructed by the entrance. Six large brick walled sheds, measuring 170 feet × 100 feet, with additional offices were built for the aircraft. Additional hangars were built as repair sheds but could also be used for storage.

The landing area was drained and reseeded but was still prone to flooding.

The main contractor was Robert McAlpine of Queensferry and the total cost of construction was £350,000. Throughout the twenties, the site became one of the main RAF flying training establishments and was later renamed RAF Sealand.

Appendix I

Aircraft Used During the First World War

Squadrons and Aircraft types stationed in Wales 1915–1919

Naval Airships
The following airships were stationed at RNAS Anglesey (Llangefni) and RNAS Pembroke (Milton) at different times.

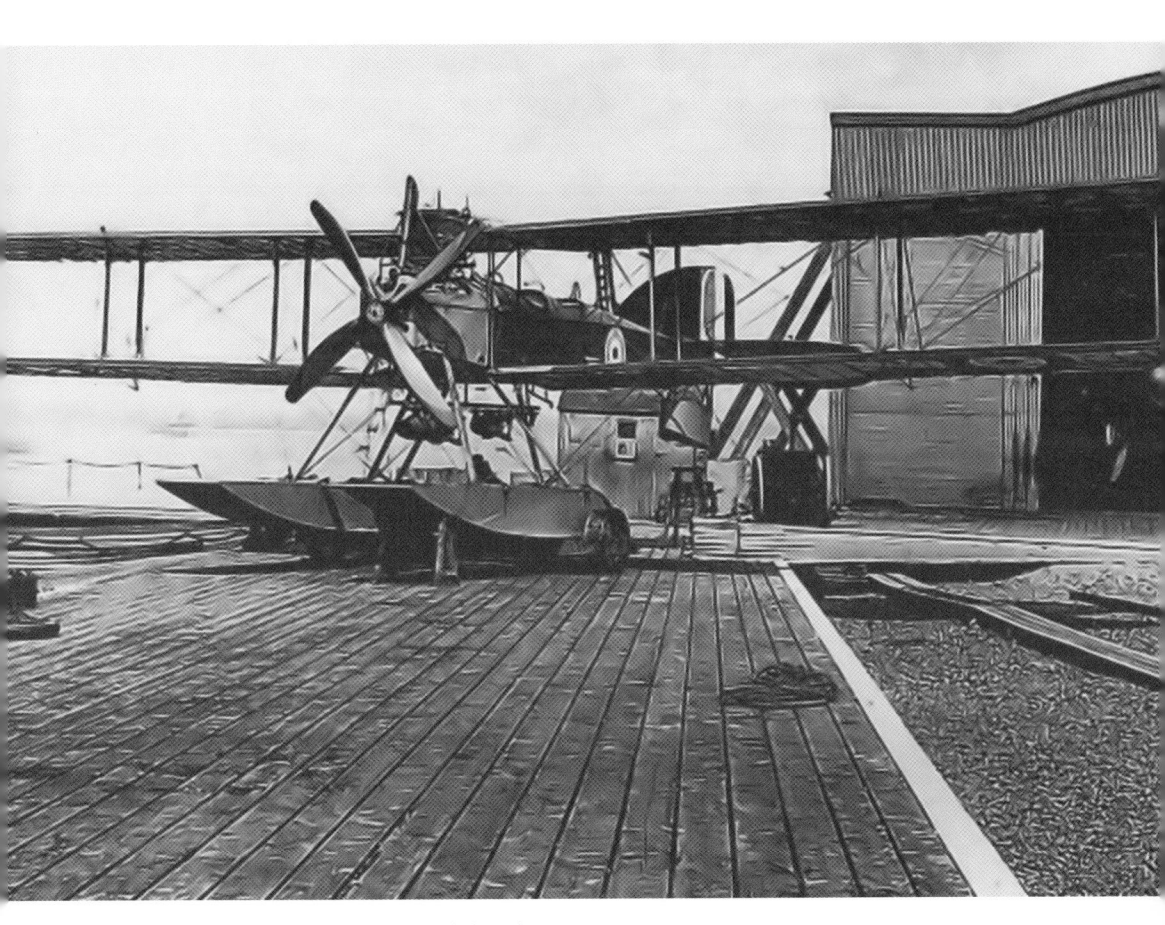

A Short Type 184 Seaplane laden with bombs.

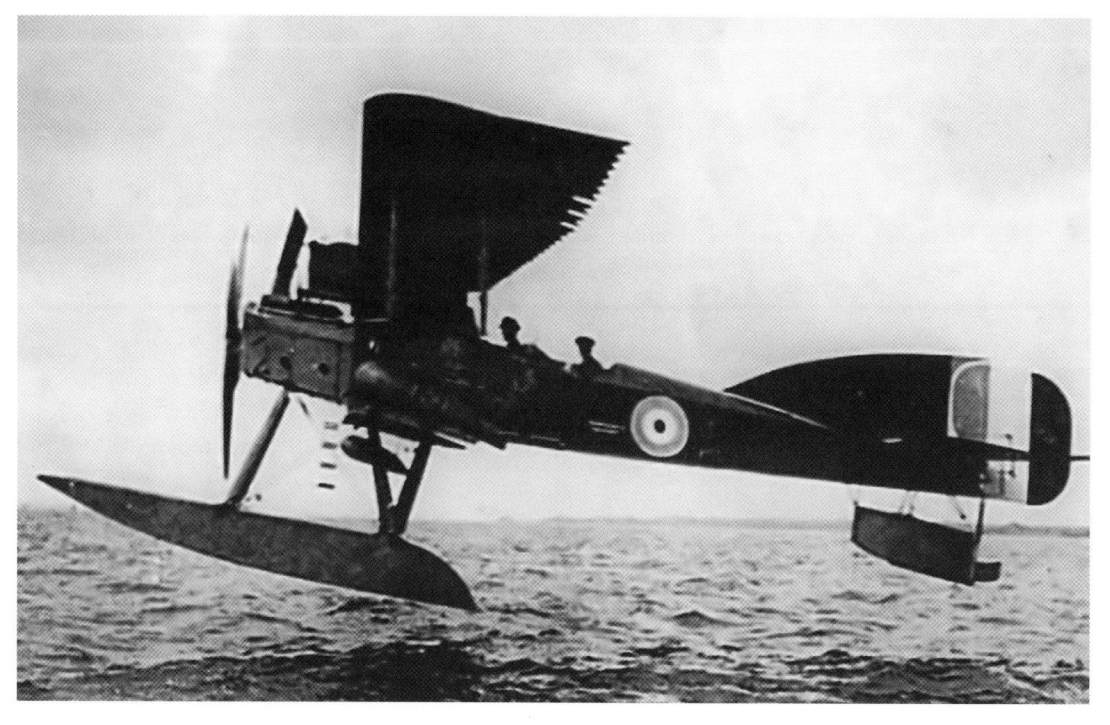

A Short 184 taking off in calm sea.

RNAS Anglesey

Sea Scout	SS-18, lost at sea 22.10.16 during an attempted landing.
	SS-22, SS-24, SS-25, SS-33 (replaced SS-18).
Sea Scout Pusher	SSP-1, SSP-6, SSP-5.
Sea Scout Zero	SSZ-31, SSZ-33, SSZ-34,
	SSZ-35, lost at sea 17.10.18.
	SSZ-50, damaged in a gale, forced-landed on beach at Aberyron, 18.11.18.
	SSZ-51, lost at sea during a patrol, 19.9.18.
	SSZ-72, SSZ-73.

RNAS Pembroke

Sea Scout	SS-15, wrecked off Lundy island, 18.6.17.
	SS-37.
	SS-42, broke away with Flight Lieutenant Monk hanging on, crashed at Ivybridge, 15.9.16.
Coastal Type	C-3.
	C-6, lost at sea because of engine failure, 23.3.17.
	C-5A.

Aircraft Used During the First World War 81

Sea Scout Zero — SSZ-16.
SSZ-17, totally destroyed by fire in a shed, 3.1.17.
SSZ-28.
SSZ-36, crashed at Capel in October, 1918.
SSZ-37, SSZ-42A, SSZ-46, SSZ-52, SSZ-53, SSZ-56.
SSZ-67, SSZ-76.

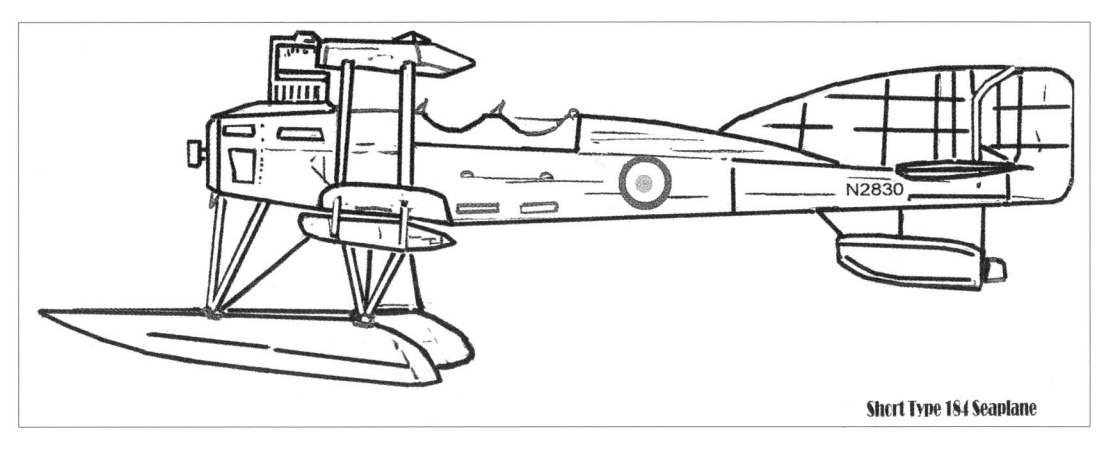

Drawing of a Short 184 seaplane.

A flying replica of a Sopwith Baby Seaplane.

RNAS/RFC squadrons and their aircraft

The following aircraft were on the squadrons inventory in 1918, admittedly a large number were unserviceable and, as usual in the military, were cannibalised for spares. Accidents became a common occurrence towards the end of the war.

No. 255 Squadron Nos 519/520 Flights

Sopwith 1½ Strutter

Eight aircraft were sent to RNAS Pembroke in April and June 1917. The Strutters were withdrawn from France and allocated to secondary duties with the Special Duties Flight. It is believed that when the Flight received DH.6s, the Strutters were kept as reserve aircraft until the Armistice.

Serial numbers not known except for one: A5277.

Airco DH.6

B2781, B2786, B2789, B2791, B2937.
B2971, suffered an engine failure was damaged during a forced landing.
B2973, B2976, B2977, B2978, B2979, B2978, B2979, B2982.
B2983, on loan from No. 256 Squadron, based at Elswick.
B3010, on loan from No. 2 Wireless School, Penhurst.
B3025, C2067.
C2074, crashed in Caernarfon Bay, 11.10.18.
C2076, C6560.
C6656, forced to ditch in the sea, 18.9.18.
C7862, C9415, C9439, C9447, C9523, F3351, F3353, F3357.

No. 244 Squadron Nos 521/522 Flights

Airco DH.4

Six DH.4 fighter-bombers were dispatched from Air Acceptance Park, Hendon, for Llangefni on 7 November 1917. Four landed at Shotwick because of bad weather. One made an emergency landing on Lavan Sands but was lost when the tide came in. The second (A7654) crashed during landing at Llangefni.

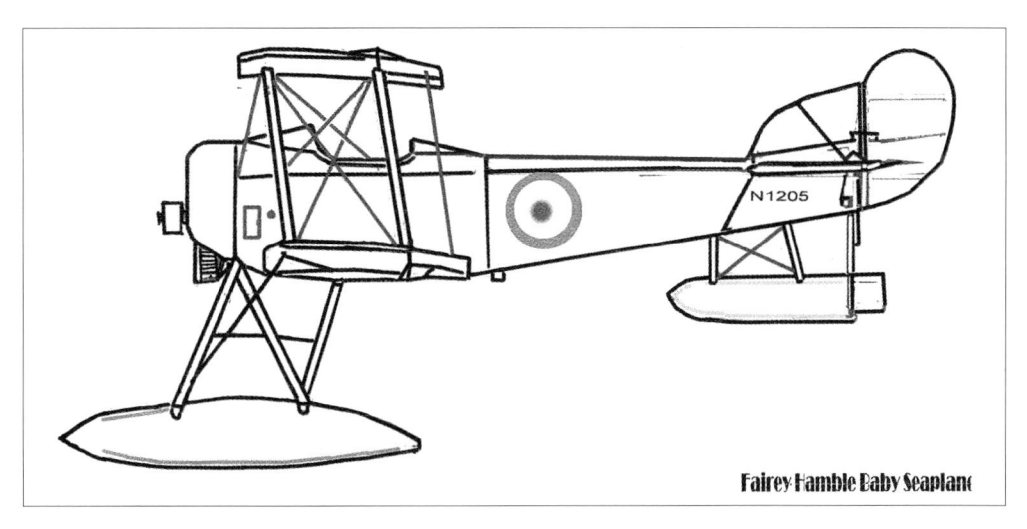

Drawing of a Fairey Hamble Baby Seaplane.

Airco DH.6

B2791, B2937.
B2971, suffered an engine failure and was damaged during a forced landing 7.9.18.
B2973, B2976, B2977, B2978, B2979, B2982.
B2983, transferred from No. 256 Squadron, based at Elswick.
B3010, on loan from No. 2 Wireless School, Penhurst.
B3023, crashed 26.8.18, spun again in 18.9.18 killing an air mechanic.
B3025.
C2021, lost at sea during a patrol on 14.12.18.
C6560, C6655, C6656.
C7861, C7862.
C7864, transferred from No. 131 Squadron, based at Shawbury.
Nos 530/520 Flight, based at Tallaght, Dublin.
C6560, C7786, C7796, C7800, C7861, C7863.
C9444, crashed at Dalkie, Dun Laoghaire, 6.11.18.

Aircraft Specifications

Sopwith 1½ Strutter

Built by the Sopwith Aircraft Company with production subcontracted out to other companies, these Sopwith fighter-bombers got their name from an unusual arrangement of short and long pairs of centre-section struts.

Powered by a single 110 hp Clerget rotary engine.
Top speed of 108 mph.
Service ceiling 10–15,000 feet.
Armed with one synchronised Vickers machine gun and a Lewis machine gun on a Scarff mounting as well as four 25-lb bombs.
Single-seater that could carry two 63-lb bombs.
First flown in December 1915, entered service in April 1916.
The 1½ Strutters were fitted with the RNAS Equal Distance Bomb Sight, which was regarded as the most sophisticated and most modern of all bomb-aiming equipment at the time.
In service with Royal Flying Corps, Royal Naval Air Service and French Military.

A single-seat Sopwith 1½ Strutter.

A Sopwith 1½ Strutter at RAF Museum, Hendon.

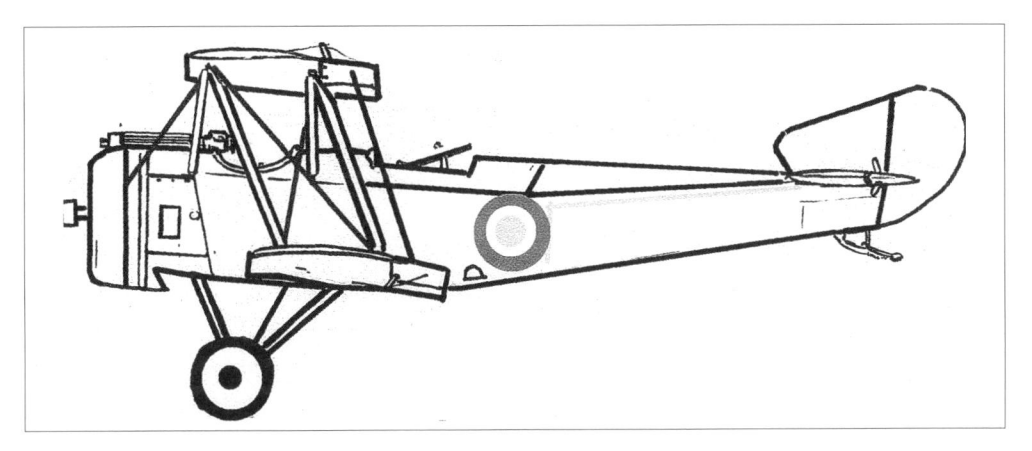

Drawing of a Sopwith 1½ Strutter.

Sopwith Baby Seaplane

This single-seat seaplane was built by Fairey, at Hamble, the Blackburn Aircraft Company at Leeds and the Parnall Manufacturing Company.

Powered by a 110 hp Clerget engine.
Top speed of 92 mph.
Endurance of two hours in reasonable weather.
Armed with a single .303 Lewis machine gun and up to 130 lbs of bombs.
First flown in 1914; entered service with RNAS in 1915 and known as Admiralty 8200 type. The Admiralty ordered 286.

The Fairey Hamble Baby was a development of the Sopwith aircraft with the ailerons replaced by a trailing edge flap, enabling the aircraft to take off and land at lower speeds, therefore reducing strain on the engine.

Airco de Havilland DH.4

Designed by Geoffrey de Havilland and built by Airco in the UK.

Airco stood for Aircraft Manufacturing Company Ltd, which was founded in 1912 and based at Hyde. Several de Havillands were built by the Westland Aircraft Company of Yeovil. A version was also built in the USA, powered by a Liberty engine.

Powered by a 375 hp Rolls-Royce Eagle engine.
Armament – one synchronised Vickers .303 machine gun.
One .303 Lewis MG on a Scarff ring mounting.
Bomb load two 230-lb bombs or four 112-lb bombs.
First flown in August 1916; entered service with the RFC in March 1917.

DH.4 was regarded as a stable and reliable light bomber and was thought to be ideally suited for coastal patrol work; nevertheless its introduction to RNAS Anglesey, north Wales was disaster.

Airco DH.6

A primary trainer aircraft designed by Geoffrey de Havilland and built by Airco.

A total of 2,280 were built in the UK and North America.
The RNAS received 300 DH.6s for coastal patrol.
Powered by a 90-hp Royal Air Force 1A V8 air-cooled engine.
Some were also powered by 80-hp Renault and 90-hp Curtiss OX5 engines (mostly those built in the USA).
Wing span – 35 feet.
Length – 27 feet.
Maximum speed – 66 mph.
Endurance – up to three hours in good weather.
Loaded weight – 2,050 lbs.

Airco DH 6

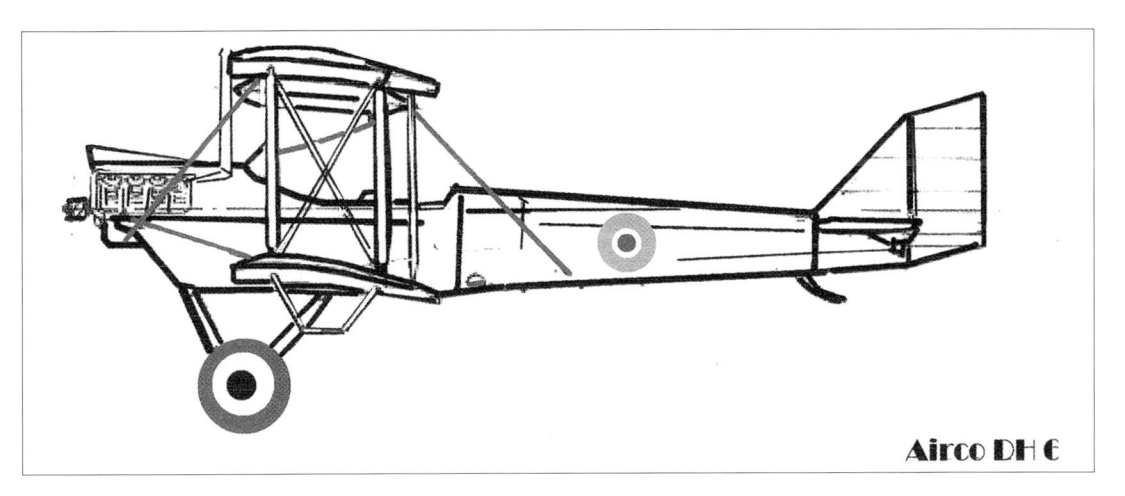

Drawing of an Airco DH.6.

Armament – up to 100-lb bomb load under the wings, or an observer was armed with .303 Lewis machine gun.

Short Type 184 Seaplane

The Short Type 184 was two-seat seaplane also referred to as Short 225.
Short also subcontracted it's manufacturing to several different companies.
Powered by a 220–240 hp Sunbeam Mohawk or Maori, or Renault engines.
Top speed of 88 mph.
Endurance up to five hours (depending on load).
Armament consisted of a .303 Lewis machine gun mounted on a Scarff or Whitehead ring mounting in the rear cockpit.
Designed to carry a 14-inch torpedo under the fuselage or up to 260 lbs of bombs.
Wing span – 63 feet.
Length – 40 feet.
Weight – 5,367 lbs.
First flown in 1915; entered service in 1915.
Total built – 536.

The airships in service with the Royal Naval Air Service

The Sea Scouts

The Admiralty issued a specification to industry on 28 February 1915 for the construction of a small airship for coastal patrols. Two companies got involved: Airship Ltd and Short Bros. E. T. Willows' envelope (the balloon) design was adopted and a BE2 aeroplane fuselage attached.

Envelope capacity – 70,000 cubic feet (after modifications).

Powered by 75-hp Renault engine, a 100-hp Berlietts or 75-hp Rolls-Royce Hawk (type of engine varied in accordance with the aircraft fuselage used).

Speed – about 50 mph with an endurance of at least eight hours.

Two-seat – pilot in the rear cockpit and the w/t operator/observer in the front.

Armaments – provision for eight 16-lb bombs, also a .303 Lewis machine gun could be installed.

SSP (Sea Scout Pusher)

Built as replacements for the SS type in 1916, but as the Zero type entered service only six were eventually built.

Envelop capacity – 70,000 cubic feet.

Length – 143 feet.

Diameter – 30 feet.

Crew of three, including a pilot, wireless operator and an engineer.

Originally powered by a 75-hp Rolls-Royce Hawk engine, later replaced by a 100-hp Greens engine.

Speed – about 47 mph and an endurance of eight hours.

Armament similar to Sea Scout series.

Coastal Class Airships

The Coastal Class was developed by using two Avro 510 seaplane fuselages joined together. The four-cockpit car was powered by two 150-hp Sunbeam engines on either end: one a tractor, the other a pusher.

The first trial flight took place on 26 May 1915 from Kingsnorth.

Further modifications were made to the airship, including upgrading the Sunbeam engines.

Later, 'Coastal's' were powered by a 220-hp Renault engine, fitted aft, and a 100-hp Berliets or Green engine forward.

Envelope capacity – 170,000 cubic feet.

Length – 196 feet.

Maximum speed was 47 mph and an endurance of 10–12 hours.

Crew of four – a coxswain in the forward cockpit, the pilot was seated behind, the wireless operator and an engineer next to the rear engine.

Armament – Two .303 Lewis machine guns and four 112-lb or two 230-lb bombs.

A Milton-based Coastal Class airship escorting a convoy in the south-western approaches. (IWM)

Photograph of a non-rigid Sea Scout Zero Class airship.

Sea Scout Zero Class

Envelope capacity – 70,000 cubic feet.
   Beam was 30 feet, with an overall height of 44 feet, 6 inches.
   Length of carriage was over 18 feet.
   Powered by an improved 75-hp Rolls-Royce Hawk water-cooled engine.
   Total fuel capacity was 102 gallons, which gave it an endurance of sixteen hours at 50 mph, or forty hours at 20 mph.
   It had a crew of three in a modified B.E.20 fuselage.
   Armament – one .303-inch Lewis machine gun, plus two 110-lb or one 250-lb bomb.

Appendix II

List of Personnel Based in Wales

List of officer air crews who served with No. 255 Squadron at any time between the formation of the squadron and its disbandment.

Pilots:
Arcand, Louis Georges. Lieutenant.
Birkbeck, Paul William. Lieutenant.
Chaffe, Redvers Sydney. 2nd Lieutenant.
Gilligham, Hubert Henry. Lieutenant.
Gould, Robert Gordon. Acting Major.
Hamilton, Ralph Nigel. Hon. Lieutenant.
Hunter, Richard Charles. 2nd Lieutenant.
Leguen-de-Lacroix, Aleth Thomas. Lieutenant.
Nicholson, Leyster. Lieutenant.
Peebles, Arthur John. Lieutenant.
Soar, Reginald Rhys. Hon. Captain.
Stallibrass, Trevor Lawrie. Lieutenant.
Tamplin, Harold Llewelyn. Lieutentant.
Observers:
Andrews, Leonard Christopher. 2nd Lieutentant
Godden, William John. 2nd Lieutenant.

Personnel who served with No. 245 squadron at RNAS Fishguard in 1918.

Commissioned Officers:
Ronald RNVR, R. J. Lieutenant.
Till, E. D. Flight Commander (later Major). CO March 1918–April 1919.
Payne, E. W. J. MC. Captain.
Woolmer, J. H. AFC. Captain.
Thomas, H. M. 2nd Lieutenant. Medical Officer.
Rich, E. J. 2nd Lieutenant. Medical Officer.

Davies RNVR, A. H. Lieutenant.
Clarke, R. G. Flight Lieutenant.
Westcott, W. G. Flight Sub-Lieutenant.
Land, F. J. Flight Sub-Lieutenant.
Alford, K. F. Flight Sub-Lieutenant.
Trotman, J. E. AFC. Flight Sub-Lieutenant.
Duckworth, C. G. Flight Sub-Lieutenant.
Helliwell, D. L. Flight Sub-Lieutenant.
Sugars, J. F. V. Observer Lieutenant.
Knowler, F. J. Warrant Officer/2nd Lieutenant.
Griffiths, W. R. M. Lieutenant.
Carr, K. H. Lieutenant.
Whitley, S. E. Lieutenant.
Foreman, D. G. Lieutenant.
Smith, E. S. Lieutenant.
Marshall, B. Lieutenant.
2nd Lieutenants:
Trinder, J. O.
Smith, T. G.
Colmer, E.
Marshall, H. L.
Stubley, T. G.
Shepperd, E. A.
Grieve, G. H.
Armes, J. O.
Fitton, A. H.
Harwood, W. F. F.
Welch, T.
Hargreaves, C.
Smith, F. W.

At the time of writing the author was unable to obtain a list of No. 244 Squadron personnel, nor personnel belonging to the airship units at Llangefni or Pembroke.

Acknowledgements

Airship Heritage Trust
Anglesey Archives
Deric Brock
CADW
Clwyd Archives
Gerry Evans
Fleet Air Arm Museum, Yeovil
Martin Hale
Holyhead Museum
Imperial War Museum, London
David Ellis-Jones (photographs and information on the airships)
Llandudno Archives
Lloyds Shipping Records
Ces Mowthorpe
The National Archives
National Museum of Wales
Pembrokeshire Archives
RNAS Association
Royal Air Force Museum, Hendon and Cosford
Mrs Ida Rowlands
Ben Turpin
No. 255 Squadron Association

Bibliography

Abbott, Patrick, *British Airships at War 1914–18* (Terence Dalton, 1989).
Brock, Deric, *Wings Over Carew* (Carew Control Tower, 1989).
Castle, Ian, *British Airships 1905–30* (Osprey Publishing, 2009).
Grant, Mike and Derrick Pratt, *Wings Across the Border: History of Aviation in North East Wales and the Northern Marches Vol. 1* (Bridge Books, 1998).
Jefford, C. G., *RAF Squadrons: A Comprehensive Record of the Movement and Equipment of All RAF Squadrons and Their Antecedents Since 1912* (Airlife Publishing Ltd, 1988).
Mowthorpe, Ces, *Battlebags: British Airships of the First World War – An Illustrated History* (Wren Park Publishers, 1998).
Phillips, Alan, *Defending Wales: The Coast and Sea Lanes in Wartime* (Amberley Publishing, 2010).
Phillips, Alan, *The Military Airfields of Wales* (Bridge Books, 2006).
Rawlings, John D. R., *Coastal Support and Special Squadrons of the RAF and their Aircraft* (June's, 1982).
Sloan, Roy, *Early Aviation in North Wales* (Gwasg Carreg Gwalch, 1989).
Tipton, John, *South Western Approaches: Air Operations from Pembrokeshire in the World Wars* (Tenby Museum, 1991).